The Blog-to-Book Blueprint

A Practical Publishing System

Richard Lowe

The Writing King

The Blog-to-Book Blueprint: A Practical Publishing System

Copyright © 2025 by Richard G Lowe

Table of Contents

Table of Contents 3

Disclaimer 6

Introduction 8

The Modern Content Landscape: Why Blog-to-Book is More
Relevant Than Ever 8

How to Use This Guide 9

Part I: Strategy 10

The Strategic Foundation 10

Content Audit and Assessment 15

Book Concept Development 20

Part II: Tactical Execution 25

Content Organization and Planning 25

The Editing Process 30

Modern Publishing Mechanics 35

Distribution and Launch Strategy 40

Part III: Use Cases and Applications 46

Business and Professional Content 46

Personal Brand and Lifestyle Content 52

Educational and How-To Content 58

Creative and Artistic Content 64

Part IV: Advanced Strategies 70

Multi-Format Content Strategy 70

Technology and Automation 75

Legal and Business Considerations 81

Part V: Execution Framework 87

The 90-Day Blog-to-Book System 87

Measuring Success and Iteration 93

Tactical Social Media Marketing 99

Collaboration Strategies 108

Advanced Monetization 118

Learning from Success and Failure: Real Case Studies 127

International Publishing Considerations 139

Conclusion 147

About the Author 150

Books by Richard Lowe 152

See books by Richard Lowe at

https://masterofworlds.com

Get free publishing insights and industry updates at

https://thewritingking.substack.com

For ghostwriting and book coaching services see

https://thewritingking.com

Disclaimer

This book gives you general information about turning blogs into books and self-publishing. Don't treat it as professional legal, tax, financial, or business advice.

Publishing laws, tax rules, platform policies, and markets change constantly. What works in one place might be illegal somewhere else. Copyright laws, contracts, royalties, and taxes differ between countries and shift without warning.

I can't guarantee this information is accurate, complete, or right for your situation. Your results will depend on your circumstances, market conditions, content quality, marketing skills, timing, and a hundred other things nobody can control.

No income guarantees here. No promises of bestseller status or early retirement. Publishing success depends on factors mostly outside your control. Those case studies and success stories? They don't predict what'll happen to you.

Platform policies change daily. Amazon, social media sites, and other services mentioned here might work completely differently by the time you read this. Features disappear, requirements change, opportunities vanish.

Tax stuff gets complicated fast, especially for international authors dealing with withholding, treaties, and reporting requirements. Get a real tax professional who knows author income and your specific mess before making money decisions.

Legal questions about contracts, copyright, fair use, and who owns what need real lawyers familiar with your situation and local laws. This general stuff can't replace actual legal advice.

Money decisions about publishing investments, business setup, and income management need real financial advisors who understand your complete financial picture.

You're responsible for your publishing decisions and whatever happens because of them. I'm not liable for any damages that come from using this information.

Introduction

You've been blogging for a while now. Maybe months, maybe years, but you've got this growing pile of content sitting there like a digital junk drawer. Every so often you scroll through your old posts and think "Hey, some of this stuff isn't terrible." Then you wonder if maybe there's a book hiding in there somewhere.

There probably is. But here's what nobody tells you about converting blog content into a book: it's not copying and pasting your greatest hits into a Word document. That's like making a gourmet meal by dumping your entire refrigerator into a blender.

The process requires real strategy, actual planning, and yes, quite a bit of new writing. When done right, turning your blog into a book establishes you as an authority in your field, creates a new revenue stream, and gives you something tangible to point to when people ask what you do for a living.

The Modern Content Landscape: Why Blog-to-Book is More Relevant Than Ever

The publishing world has changed dramatically since the early days of blogging. Self-publishing platforms have matured, print-on-demand technology has eliminated massive upfront investments, and readers accept books from non-traditional publishers.

> ★ Pro Tip: Amazon's Kindle Direct Publishing handles more than half of all book sales in many categories. Your blog-to-book project has the same distribution potential as traditionally published works.

Content creators are building audiences across multiple platforms. Your blog readers might follow you on LinkedIn, subscribe to your newsletter, and listen to your podcast. A book becomes the natural evolution of this relationship, offering deeper value than any single blog post could provide.

The attention economy has shifted in ways that favor book authors. While everyone fights for seconds of attention on social media, books still command hours of focused engagement. When someone buys your book, they're committing to spend serious time with your ideas.

> ▲ Caution: Not every blog should become a book. Quality and coherence matter more than quantity of posts.

How to Use This Guide

This book follows a logical progression from big-picture strategy through tactical execution to specific use cases and advanced techniques. Each section builds on the previous one, but experienced content creators can jump around based on their specific needs.

The strategic section helps you think through whether your blog content is book-worthy and how to position it in the market. The tactical chapters walk you through the nuts and bolts of organizing, editing, and publishing your content. The use cases section shows how different types of bloggers have successfully made the transition, and the advanced strategies cover the business and technical aspects most people don't think about until they're knee-deep in the process.

You'll find real examples from successful blog-to-book conversions, specific tools and resources that can speed up your workflow, and honest assessments of what works and what doesn't. The goal isn't to convince you that everyone should write a book, but to give you the information you need to decide if it makes sense for your situation and how to execute it properly if you move forward.

> ■ Danger Zone: Don't try to implement everything at once. Pick one approach, execute it completely, then consider expanding your strategy.

Part I: Strategy

The Strategic Foundation

"Most people don't have the guts to admit they're trying to build a media empire from their bathroom blog posts. I respect that kind of self-delusion." - Anonymous Publishing Executive

---

Defining Your Book's Purpose Beyond "I Have Blog Posts"

Let's get this out of the way first: having a bunch of blog posts doesn't automatically mean you should write a book. Shocking, I know. The internet is littered with digital corpses of bloggers who thought quantity equals quality and slapped together their archives into something they generously called a "book."

Your book needs a reason to exist beyond "I wrote some stuff and people seemed to like it." Real purpose comes from solving a problem for a group of people. Maybe you've been blogging about freelance writing for three years and figured out the exact system that takes someone from zero to six-figure income. That's a book. Maybe you've been documenting your journey through startup failures and identified the five mistakes that kill 90% of new businesses. Also a book.

> ★ Pro Tip: The strongest book purposes answer this question: "After reading this, what will someone be able to do that they couldn't do before?"

The worst book purposes sound like this: "I want to share my thoughts on leadership" or "I have insights about marketing." Those aren't purposes, they're vague gestures in the direction of importance. Your blog might cover leadership, but your book needs to teach someone how to lead a remote team through a crisis, or how to transition from individual contributor to manager without losing their mind.

Purpose determines everything else about your book. It shapes which blog posts make the cut, what new content you need to write, how you organize the material, and who you're writing for. Without clear purpose, you'll end up with a collection of related essays that feel more like a magazine than a cohesive book.

Understanding Your Audience: Blog Readers vs. Book Buyers

Here's where things get interesting. The people who read your blog for free are not the same people who will pay $15 for your book. Blog readers are browsers. They're checking you out, seeing if you know what you're talking about, getting quick hits of information or entertainment. Book buyers are investors. They're making a commitment to spend hours with your ideas and they expect a return on that investment.

Your blog audience might love your quick tips and random observations, but book buyers want systems, frameworks, and comprehensive solutions. They don't want to know that "consistency is important in content marketing." They want to know exactly how to create 90 days of content in advance, how to maintain quality when posting daily, and what to do when they run out of ideas.

> ▲ Caution: Don't assume your most popular blog posts will translate directly to the best book chapters. Viral content often works because it's surprising or controversial, not because it's deeply useful.

The overlap between your blog audience and book audience is real, but smaller than you think. Your book needs to work for people who have never read your blog. It needs to stand alone as a complete resource. This means more context, more explanation, and more hand-holding than your blog posts provide.

Book buyers have different consumption patterns too. They might read your book in chunks over several weeks, or binge the whole thing on a weekend. They might skip around to chapters that interest them most, or read cover to cover. Your blog posts can assume people are reading them in order and remember what you said last week. Your book can't make those assumptions.

Positioning Your Book in the Market

Every book category on Amazon is a battlefield, and you need to know what you're walking into. Your positioning determines whether you're competing against Malcolm Gladwell or the guy who self-published his first book last Tuesday. Both are valid strategies, but they require completely different approaches.

If you're positioning yourself as the definitive guide to something, you're competing against established authorities and well-funded traditional publishers. You better have credentials, case studies, and content that's genuinely superior to what's already available. If you're positioning yourself as the accessible, practical alternative to academic or overly complex resources, you can compete on clarity and relatability instead of authority.

Market positioning starts with understanding what already exists. Spend time browsing the categories where your book would live. Look at the top sellers, read their descriptions, check out their table of contents, and read the reviews. Pay attention to what reviewers complain about. Those complaints are opportunities for your book to be better.

★ Pro Tip: Amazon's "Customers who bought this item also bought" section is a goldmine for understanding your competitive landscape and identifying adjacent markets.

Your blog gives you a huge advantage in positioning because you already know what resonates with people. You can see which posts get the most engagement, which topics generate the most questions, and where existing resources fall short. Use that data to position your book as the solution to problems other books don't address.

Positioning isn't just about competitors though. It's about setting expectations. Are you writing the comprehensive reference guide that people will keep on their desk for years? Are you writing the inspiring kick-in-the-pants that people will recommend to friends? Are you writing the step-by-step manual that walks someone through a process? Each positioning requires different content, different organization, and different marketing.

The Economics of Blog-to-Book Conversion

Let's talk money, because someone has to. Converting your blog to a book isn't just a creative endeavor, it's a business decision. You're investing time, energy, and probably some money into creating something you hope will generate income for years to come.

The math on self-published books is straightforward but not encouraging. Most self-published books sell fewer than 100 copies. The ones that do well sell between 1,000 and 10,000 copies over their lifetime. At $2-5 profit per book (depending on price and format), you're looking at $2,000 to $50,000 in lifetime revenue.

That might sound disappointing until you consider the indirect benefits. A book establishes credibility in ways that blog posts can't. It opens doors to speaking opportunities, consulting gigs, and media appearances. It gives you something to offer as a lead magnet or bonus for higher-value products. Many successful authors make more money from opportunities their book creates than from book sales themselves.

■ Danger Zone: Don't quit your day job based on projected book sales. Even successful books take months or years to build momentum.

The investment side varies dramatically based on how much work you do yourself. If you're writing, editing, designing, and marketing the book yourself, your main investment is time. If you're hiring professionals for editing, cover design, and marketing, you could easily spend $5,000 to $15,000 before you sell a single copy.

Your blog gives you a head start on the economics because you already have an audience and a content foundation. You're not starting from zero like most first-time authors. You have people who already know and trust your work, and you have proven content that resonates with readers. That's worth more than most authors realize.

The key is being realistic about timelines and expectations. Your book probably won't make you rich, but it can be a profitable part of a larger content and business strategy. Think of it as a long-term investment in your authority and influence, not a get-rich-quick scheme.

"Looking back at your old blog posts is like going through your high school yearbook. Half of it makes you cringe, a quarter of it is surprisingly good, and the rest you have no memory of writing." - Content Creator Anonymous

---

Evaluating Your Existing Content for Book Potential

Time for the fun part: digging through your digital archives like an archaeologist searching for buried treasure. Except instead of ancient pottery, you're looking for blog posts that don't make you want to delete your entire online presence.

Start by pulling every single post you've ever published. Yes, even the ones from 2019 when you thought writing in Comic Sans was edgy. You need to see the full scope of what you're working with before you can make any decisions about what belongs in a book.

The first pass is brutal but necessary. Read through everything with fresh eyes and sort your posts into three piles: "This is good," "This could be good with work," and "What was I thinking?" Be honest here. Your blog readers might have been polite about that rambling 3,000-word post about your coffee preferences, but book buyers won't be.

> ★ Pro Tip: Read your posts as if you're seeing them for the first time. If you have to explain why something is interesting or important, it probably isn't book material.

Look for posts that solve real problems, teach concrete skills, or provide frameworks people can apply immediately. The best blog-to-book content answers questions like "How do I..." or "What should I do when..." The worst content answers questions nobody asked, like "What do I think about industry trends?"

Pay attention to posts that generated unusual engagement. Comments, shares, and responses from readers are gold mines of information about what resonates. But don't confuse viral with valuable. That post about your worst client experience might have gotten a million views, but unless it contains practical advice about avoiding similar situations, it's entertainment, not book material.

Identifying Themes and Natural Groupings

Once you've separated the wheat from the chaff, patterns start emerging. Maybe you realize you've been circling around the same five topics for years. Maybe you notice that your most helpful posts all deal with beginner-level problems. Maybe you discover you've written a complete guide to something without realizing it.

Look for natural clusters where posts build on each other or address different aspects of the same challenge. If you've been blogging about freelance writing, you might have clusters around finding clients, setting rates, managing projects, and dealing with difficult customers. Each cluster could become a section of your book.

> ▲ Caution: Don't force connections that aren't there. If a post doesn't fit naturally into your emerging themes, it might be better suited for a different book or no book at all.

The strongest themes solve progression problems. Your readers start at point A and want to get to point B, and your posts map out the journey between them. Maybe point A is "I want to start a podcast" and point B is "I have a successful show with sponsors." Your blog posts probably cover equipment, recording techniques, distribution, audience building, and monetization. That's a book right there.

Weaker themes are collections of loosely related observations. You might have fifty posts about marketing, but if they don't connect to form a coherent system or approach, you don't have a book theme. You have a marketing blog.

Timeline matters too. Look at how your thinking has evolved. Your early posts might reflect outdated thinking or approaches you've since abandoned. Your recent posts might represent your current best practices. A good book synthesizes the journey and presents the refined version of your ideas.

Gap Analysis: What's Missing for a Complete Book

This is where reality hits. You've got some great content, you've identified themes, and you're feeling pretty good about your book prospects. Then you start mapping out what a complete book would look like and realize you're missing half the pieces.

Gap analysis means looking at your content clusters and asking what else someone would need to go from beginner to success in your topic area. You might have great content about advanced techniques but nothing for people just starting out. You might have tons of strategic advice but no tactical implementation guides. You might cover the happy path but ignore what happens when things go wrong.

Think about your book as a complete system, not a collection of related articles. What questions will readers have that your existing posts don't answer? What steps in the process have you skipped because they seemed obvious to you? What assumptions are you making about what readers already know?

★ Pro Tip: Look at the comments on your posts for questions you didn't think to address. Reader questions reveal gaps in your content better than any analysis you can do yourself.

Some gaps are easy to fill with new content. If you're missing a beginner's guide to getting started, you can write one. If you need more examples or case studies, you can create them. Other gaps might reveal that you don't have enough material for a complete book yet, or that you need to narrow your focus to what you can cover thoroughly.

The worst thing you can do is ignore the gaps and hope readers won't notice. They will notice, and they'll feel like they bought an incomplete product. Better to write a focused book that covers one area completely than a broad book that leaves readers hanging.

Quality vs. Quantity: Choosing Your Best Material

Here's where most bloggers go wrong: they think more content makes a better book. Wrong. Dead wrong. A book with ten great chapters beats a book with twenty mediocre chapters every single time.

Your blog might have 200 posts, but your book should probably use content from fewer than 50 of them. Quality beats quantity in every measurable way. Readers would pay for concentrated value over diluted wisdom.

Start with your absolute best content and work backwards. What are the posts you're genuinely proud of? What content do people still reference months or years after you published it? What posts have you returned to yourself when you needed to remember how to do something?

> ▲ Caution: Don't include content just because it took you a long time to write. Effort doesn't equal value.

Be ruthless about cutting content that doesn't meet your quality bar. That post about productivity hacks might be perfectly fine, but if it's not as strong as your other material, it doesn't belong in the book. Every piece of content in your book should justify its inclusion.

Length isn't quality either. Some of your best insights might come from short posts, while some of your longest posts might be rambling messes that could be condensed into two paragraphs. Judge content by impact, not word count.

The goal is to create something where every chapter makes readers think "I'm glad I bought this book." If any chapter makes them think "This feels like filler," you've failed. Better to have a shorter book that delivers consistent value than a longer book that tests readers' patience.

> ■ Danger Zone: Don't try to include everything you've ever learned about a topic. Focus on what readers need most, not what you know most about.

This isn't your last book. You don't have to cram every insight you've ever had into this project. Save some material for future books, courses, or blog posts. Your readers will thank you for the focused approach, and you'll thank yourself when you have material for your next project.

Book Concept Development

"The difference between a collection of blog posts and a book is the same as the difference between a pile of bricks and a house. Same materials, completely different purpose." - Publishing veteran overheard at a coffee shop

From Blog Archive to Cohesive Narrative

Your blog posts weren't written to become a book. They were written to solve individual problems, answer specific questions, or share particular insights. Each post stands alone, complete in itself. Books don't work that way.

A book needs an overarching story that carries readers from the beginning to the end. Not a literal story with characters and plot twists, but a narrative arc that makes sense of why chapter three comes after chapter two and why the conclusion feels inevitable given everything that came before.

Think of your favorite business or self-help books. The best ones don't just present information, they take you on a journey. You start as one kind of person and finish as another. You begin with certain assumptions and end with different ones. You have problems at the beginning that are solved by the end.

Your blog posts probably contain all the ingredients for this kind of transformation, but they're scattered across months or years of writing. Your job is to find the through-line that connects them into something larger than the sum of their parts.

Creating Original Value Beyond Republished Posts

Here's what separates amateur blog-to-book conversions from professional ones: the amount of new content. Amateurs copy and paste their posts into chapters and call it done.

Professionals use their posts as raw material for something entirely new.

> ★ Pro Tip: Plan to write at least 30% new content for your book, even if you're starting with strong blog material. This new content will be what holds everything together.

Blog posts assume certain knowledge and skip certain explanations because your regular readers already know your background and approach. Book readers don't have that context. They need more setup, more explanation, and more connection between ideas.

You'll also need to write transitions that didn't exist in your original posts. When you published a post about email marketing in March and a post about social media strategy in June, you didn't need to explain how they relate to each other. In a book, those connections need to be explicit.

New content also gives you the chance to update and improve your thinking. Maybe you've learned something since you wrote that post two years ago. Maybe you've seen how your advice works in practice and want to refine it. Maybe you have better examples or clearer explanations now.

> ▲ Caution: Don't get so caught up in creating new content that you lose sight of what made your original posts valuable in the first place.

The best new content serves the book's overall purpose while enhancing the existing material. Introductions that set up what's coming. Conclusions that tie together what you've covered. Case studies that illustrate points you only touched on in blog posts. Frameworks that organize information scattered across multiple posts.

Structuring for Different Reader Types

Not everyone will read your book the same way. Some people read business books cover to cover like novels. Others skip around to the chapters that interest them most. Still others use books as reference materials, returning to specific sections when they need help with particular problems.

Your structure needs to work for all these reading styles without sacrificing coherence for any of them. This means each chapter should stand alone while contributing to the larger narrative. It means your introduction should orient all readers, not just the ones who plan to read every word.

Consider your reader's situation when they pick up your book. Are they facing an immediate crisis and looking for quick solutions? Are they planning ahead and trying to avoid future problems? Are they beginners who need everything explained, or experts who want advanced strategies?

Your blog analytics probably tell you a lot about how people consume your content. Do they read your posts in order, or jump around based on what they need? Do they come back to reference old posts, or read once and move on? Do they share certain types of content more than others?

> ■ Danger Zone: Don't try to serve every possible reader type equally. Choose your primary audience and structure for them, then accommodate other reading styles where possible.

The most successful blog-to-book conversions have a clear primary path through the material while offering multiple entry points for different needs. Maybe your main narrative takes beginners from zero to competence, but you include advanced tips and shortcuts for experienced readers who want to skip ahead.

Setting Realistic Scope and Timeline

This is where most blog-to-book projects die. Authors get excited about their concept and set unrealistic expectations about how much work is involved or how quickly they can complete it.

Writing a book from scratch typically takes 6-12 months for experienced authors. Converting blog content into a book should be faster since you're starting with existing material, but it's still a substantial project. Plan for 3-6 months of focused work, depending on how much new content you need to create and how much editing your existing posts require.

Scope creep kills more book projects than any other factor. You start with a focused idea about freelance writing, then decide you should also cover client management, then think you need a section on business development, then realize you haven't covered taxes and accounting. Before you know it, you're trying to write the definitive guide to running a freelance business instead of a focused book about writing.

★ Pro Tip: Write your one-sentence book description before you do anything else, and refer back to it whenever you're tempted to expand the scope.

Your first book doesn't need to cover everything you know about your topic. In fact, it shouldn't. Focused books are better books. They're easier to write, easier to market, and more valuable to readers than comprehensive guides that try to be everything to everyone.

Timeline pressure also affects quality. If you're rushing to hit an arbitrary deadline, you'll make compromises that hurt the final product. Better to take the time needed to create something you're proud of than to rush out something that feels half-finished.

Remember that publishing your book is just the beginning, not the end. You'll need time for marketing, promotion, and building on the platform your book creates. Don't exhaust yourself on the writing phase that you have no energy left for everything that comes after.

The best approach is to set conservative timelines and realistic scope, then be pleasantly surprised if you finish early or discover you can cover more ground than expected. This beats

the alternative of setting aggressive goals and burning out
halfway through.

Part II: Tactical Execution

Content Organization and Planning

"Organizing blog posts into a book is like trying to build IKEA furniture without the instruction manual. You have all the pieces, but good luck figuring out what goes where." - Frustrated author on a writing forum

---

Mapping Blog Posts to Book Structure

Now comes the part where you stare at a spreadsheet full of blog post titles and try to make sense of how they fit together. It's like doing a jigsaw puzzle where half the pieces are from different boxes and some idiot threw away the picture on the front.

Start by printing out (yes, printing) a one-line summary of each blog post you're considering for the book. Spread them out on a table or tape them to a wall. Digital organization tools are great, but sometimes you need to physically move pieces around to see patterns that aren't obvious on a screen.

Group related posts together without worrying about perfect categories yet. You're looking for natural clusters, not forcing posts into predetermined buckets. Maybe you discover that posts you thought were about different topics are all addressing the same underlying problem. Maybe posts you assumed belonged together are solving completely different challenges.

> ▲ Caution: Don't try to use every good post you've ever written. Some excellent content won't fit your book's narrative, and that's fine.

Look for progression within your clusters. Do the posts in each group follow a logical sequence from basic to advanced? Do they build on each other, or are they parallel approaches to the same problem? The best book sections take readers on a journey, not just dump information on them.

You'll probably discover gaps where the logical flow breaks down. Maybe you have great posts about getting started and advanced techniques, but nothing about the messy middle phase where people get stuck. Flag these gaps now because you'll need to write new content to fill them.

Creating Bridges Between Existing Content

Your blog posts were written months or years apart, for different occasions, in response to different questions. They weren't designed to flow smoothly from one to the next. Making them work together requires building bridges between ideas that were never meant to connect.

Some bridges are simple transitions that acknowledge the shift from one topic to another. "Now that you understand how to find clients, let's talk about what happens when they find you." Other bridges require more substantial content that explains relationships between concepts that weren't obvious in the original posts.

★ Pro Tip: Read your organized posts in sequence as if you're encountering the ideas for the first time. Where do you get confused or feel like something is missing? Those are your bridge opportunities.

The trickiest bridges connect posts written at different stages of your own learning. That post you wrote two years ago when you were figuring things out might contradict the post you wrote last month when you had more experience. Don't just ignore the contradiction. Address it directly and explain how your thinking has evolved.

Sometimes you'll need to completely rewrite the beginning or end of a post to make it flow with the surrounding content. A blog post that starts with "I've been thinking about productivity lately" might need to start with "The framework from the previous chapter works great until you hit your first major deadline crunch" when it becomes part of a book.

Bridge content is often where your personality as an author shines through most clearly. These aren't recycled blog posts, they're fresh writing that reflects your current thinking and ties your ideas together in ways that weren't possible when you were writing individual posts.

Writing New Material to Fill Gaps

Gap-filling content falls into several categories, and each requires a different approach. You might need foundational content that brings beginners up to speed, advanced content that serves experienced readers, or connecting content that links different sections of your book.

Foundational gaps are the easiest to identify but sometimes the hardest to write. You know your topic so well that explaining the basics feels obvious and boring. But beginners need this content, and they need it to be engaging, not just functional. The best foundational content doesn't just explain what to do, it explains why it matters and what happens if you skip it.

Advanced gaps require you to push beyond what you've covered in your blog. Maybe your posts focus on tactics but your book needs strategic thinking. Maybe your blog covers the happy path but your book needs troubleshooting advice. This new content often becomes the most valuable part of your book because it's knowledge you haven't shared anywhere else.

> ■ Danger Zone: Don't write filler content just to hit a target word count. Every new piece should serve the book's purpose and help readers achieve their goals.

Connecting content requires you to think about your topic at a higher level than individual blog posts demand. How do the different aspects of your subject relate to each other? What's the underlying system that ties everything together? This meta-level thinking often produces insights that wouldn't have emerged from just collecting existing posts.

When writing new content, resist the temptation to match the style and structure of your original blog posts exactly. Blog posts and book chapters serve different purposes and can have different voices. Your new content should feel cohesive with the existing material while taking advantage of the book format's strengths.

Maintaining Voice Consistency Across Time Periods

Here's a problem nobody warns you about: your writing voice probably changed between your first blog post and your most recent one. Maybe you've gotten more confident, more casual, or more focused. Maybe you've developed stronger opinions or learned to explain things more clearly. Your book needs to sound like it was written by one person at one point in time, not a collection of different versions of yourself.

The solution isn't to rewrite everything in your current voice, which would be a massive undertaking and might strip away some of the authenticity that made your original posts compelling. Instead, you need to find the through-line that connects all versions of your voice and emphasize that consistency.

Look for elements that have remained constant in your writing. Maybe you've always used certain types of examples or maintained a particular attitude toward your subject. Maybe your core principles haven't changed even if your expression of them has evolved. These consistent elements become the foundation for your book's voice.

★ Pro Tip: Read your selected posts aloud to identify voice inconsistencies that aren't obvious when reading silently. Your ear will catch awkward transitions that your eye might miss.

Some voice evolution benefits your book. If your early posts were tentative and your recent ones are more authoritative, that progression can mirror your reader's journey from uncertainty to confidence. Frame the evolution as part of the story instead of trying to hide it.

The new content you write will naturally reflect your current voice, so use it strategically to smooth over inconsistencies in the older material. A strong introduction written in your current style can set expectations for the entire book. Transitions and conclusions written now can help tie together content from different periods.

Voice consistency also means being consistent about your relationship with the reader. Are you the expert teaching the student, the experienced practitioner sharing with peers, or the fellow traveler reporting from further down the path? Your blog posts might have used different relationships at different times, but your book needs to pick one and stick with it.

The Editing Process

"Editing is like performing surgery on your own brain while you're still using it. Painful, necessary, and you're never quite sure if you're making things better or worse." - Editor's confession in a late-night email

---

First Pass: Content Selection and Arrangement

Welcome to the bloodbath. This is where you take all that carefully organized content and start cutting it apart like a deranged film editor. Your goal isn't to preserve every precious word you've ever written. Your goal is to create something that doesn't make readers want to throw your book across the room.

Start by reading everything in sequence, as if you're a reader encountering these ideas for the first time. Don't edit for grammar or style yet. Just focus on flow and logic. Does each section lead naturally to the next? Do you repeat yourself unnecessarily? Do you contradict yourself by accident?

> ★ Pro Tip: Print out your entire manuscript and read it away from your computer. It's easier to see big-picture problems when you're not tempted to start fixing every little thing.

Mark sections that feel redundant, confusing, or tangential. Be brutal. That clever analogy you love might be derailing your main argument. That detailed case study might be overkill when a simple example would work. That personal anecdote might be more about you than about helping your readers.

Look for places where you assume knowledge your readers might not have. Blog readers who have been following you for months might understand your shorthand, but book readers starting fresh need more context. Flag these spots for expansion in the next pass.

Pay attention to pacing too. Some sections might rush through complex ideas too quickly. Others might belabor simple points until readers get impatient. You want a rhythm that keeps people engaged without overwhelming them.

Second Pass: Rewriting for Book Format

Blog posts and book chapters are different animals. Blog posts can start abruptly, jump around, and end without much resolution because readers expect a casual, conversational experience. Book chapters need stronger structure, clearer progression, and more satisfying conclusions.

This is where you transform your blog voice into your book voice. Not completely different, but more polished and purposeful. You're still the same person with the same perspective, but you're presenting your ideas in a more organized, comprehensive way.

> ▲ Caution: Don't over-edit your personality out of the content. Readers chose your book partly because they connected with your voice on your blog.

Start each chapter with a clear statement of what you're going to cover and why it matters. End each chapter with a summary of key points and a preview of what's coming next. This might feel repetitive compared to your blog style, but book readers appreciate signposts that help them navigate longer content.

Expand abbreviated explanations that made sense in blog posts but need more detail in a book. If you wrote "Use the framework I described last month," you now need to either repeat the framework or provide a clear reference to where readers can find it.

Cut or revise insider references that won't make sense to people who haven't been following your blog. "As I mentioned in my post about difficult clients" becomes "When dealing with difficult clients" or gets expanded into a proper explanation.

Some of your blog content will need to be completely rewritten to fit the book's structure and purpose. Don't be afraid to throw out paragraphs or even entire sections if they're not serving the book's goals.

Third Pass: Professional Polish

Now you get to be picky about word choice, sentence structure, and all the technical details that make the difference between amateur and professional writing. This is where you catch the typos, fix the awkward phrasing, and smooth out the rough edges.

Read everything aloud again. Your ear will catch problems that your eye misses. Sentences that look fine on paper might be tongue twisters when spoken. Paragraphs that seem well-organized might have jarring rhythm problems when you hear them.

> ■ Danger Zone: Don't get so focused on perfecting individual sentences that you lose sight of whether the overall chapter works. Polish is pointless if the foundation is shaky.

Look for repetitive word choices and varied sentence structures. If every paragraph starts the same way or every sentence follows the same pattern, your writing will feel monotonous. Mix short punchy sentences with longer, more complex ones.

Check your transitions between paragraphs and sections. Do they help readers follow your logic, or are they just filler words that add nothing? Good transitions either show relationships between ideas or signal shifts in direction.

Pay attention to your examples and analogies. Do they clarify your points, or are they just decorative? Do they connect to your readers' experiences, or are they too tied to your own situation?

This is also where you verify facts, check statistics, and make sure your advice is current and accurate. Nothing kills credibility faster than outdated information or obvious errors.

Working with Editors vs. Self-Editing

Here's the uncomfortable truth: you can't edit your own work as well as someone else can. You're too close to the material, too invested in your original choices, and too likely to miss problems that would be obvious to fresh eyes.

Professional editing comes in several flavors. Developmental editing focuses on big-picture issues like structure, content, and organization. Copy editing tackles grammar, style, and consistency. Proofreading catches typos and formatting errors. You might need all three, or you might be able to handle some yourself.

If you're working with a tight budget, invest in developmental editing first. It's better to have a well-structured book with some typos than a perfectly polished book that doesn't make sense. You can catch most grammar and spelling errors yourself if you're careful, but structural problems require outside perspective.

★ Pro Tip: If you can't afford professional editing, find beta readers who represent your target audience. Their feedback won't replace professional editing, but it will catch problems you can't see.

When working with editors, be clear about what you want. Are you looking for someone to fix your grammar, or someone to challenge your arguments? Are you open to major structural changes, or do you just want polishing? Different editors have different strengths and different approaches.

Good editors will push back on your choices and suggest changes that might make you uncomfortable initially. That's their job. Bad editors will either accept everything uncritically or try to rewrite your book in their own voice. Learn the difference.

If you're self-editing, take breaks between passes. Work on other projects for a week or two, then come back to your manuscript with fresher eyes. Distance helps you see problems that familiarity obscures.

Self-editing also means being honest about your weaknesses as a writer. Are you prone to run-on sentences? Do you overuse certain words? Do you explain things in the right order? Knowing your tendencies helps you watch for problems.

The goal isn't perfection, it's clarity and professionalism. Your book needs to communicate your ideas effectively without distracting readers with errors or confusion. Focus on serving your readers, not impressing other writers.

Modern Publishing Mechanics

Self-Publishing Platforms: Amazon, IngramSpark, and Beyond

Amazon owns the game, and everyone else is playing for scraps. Kindle Direct Publishing handles roughly 70% of all ebook sales and a big chunk of print-on-demand paperbacks. You can fight this reality or embrace it, but you can't ignore it.

KDP is where most first-time authors should start. The interface is straightforward, the royalty structure is transparent, and you can have your book available worldwide within 24 hours of uploading. The learning curve is manageable, and the mistakes you make won't cost you much money.

But Amazon isn't your only option, and putting all your eggs in one basket has risks. IngramSpark gives you access to bookstores and libraries that Amazon doesn't reach. Draft2Digital distributes to multiple platforms with a single upload. Smashwords has been around forever and still serves markets that newer platforms ignore.

★ Pro Tip: Start with Amazon to test your book and work out the kinks, then expand to other platforms once you've proven there's demand for your content.

Each platform has its quirks and requirements. Amazon wants your book exclusively for maximum royalties but gives you less control over pricing and distribution. IngramSpark offers wider distribution but requires more technical knowledge and charges setup fees. Draft2Digital simplifies multi-platform publishing but takes a larger cut of your royalties.

The technical requirements vary too. File formats, cover dimensions, margin settings, and metadata requirements differ between platforms. What works perfectly on Amazon might need adjustments for IngramSpark. Plan for this complexity instead of assuming one file will work everywhere.

Don't get paralyzed by platform choice. Pick one, learn it thoroughly, and get your book published. You can always expand to other platforms later, but you can't sell books that exist only in your head.

Print vs. Digital vs. Audio Considerations

Your blog readers might consume content on their phones during coffee breaks, but book buyers have different preferences. Some want physical books they can highlight and dog-ear. Others prefer ebooks they can read on any device. A growing number want audiobooks they can listen to during commutes.

> ▲ Caution: Don't assume your audience wants the same format you prefer. Check what's selling in your category and price range.

Ebooks are the easiest to produce and have the highest profit margins. No printing costs, no shipping delays, no inventory management. You upload a file and start selling immediately. But ebook sales have plateaued in many categories while print sales have grown.

Print books require more planning and higher upfront costs, but they feel more substantial to buyers and command higher prices. A $2.99 ebook might become a $12.99 paperback with similar profit margins once you account for production costs.

Print-on-demand has eliminated most of the traditional barriers to physical book publishing. You don't need to order thousands of copies or rent warehouse space. Books are printed only when someone orders them, shipped directly to customers, and you never touch the inventory.

Audiobooks represent the fastest-growing segment of the book market, but they're also the most expensive to produce. Professional narration can cost $5,000 to $15,000 for a typical business book. Self-narration is cheaper but requires time investment and technical skill.

> ■ Danger Zone: Don't try to launch in all formats simultaneously unless you have substantial resources. Master one format first, then expand.

Format choice affects more than just production. Different formats attract different readers and command different prices. Ebook readers tend to be price-sensitive and read quickly. Print book buyers are often gift-givers or people who want permanent reference materials. Audiobook listeners are usually busy professionals who consume content during other activities.

ISBN, Copyright, and Legal Requirements

ISBNs are like social security numbers for books. They identify your edition and format to retailers, libraries, and distributors. Amazon will assign a free ISBN if you don't have one, but using their ISBN means Amazon is listed as the publisher, not you.

Buying your own ISBNs gives you more control and credibility, but it's not strictly necessary for most self-published authors. If you plan to publish multiple books or want bookstores to take you seriously, invest in your own ISBNs. If you just want to test the waters with one book, Amazon's free option works fine.

Copyright protection exists automatically when you create original content, but registering your copyright with the U.S. Copyright Office provides additional legal protections. For most blog-to-book conversions, automatic copyright is sufficient unless you're concerned about piracy or plan to license your content.

> ★ Pro Tip: Include a proper copyright page in your book even if you don't register the copyright. It makes your book look professional and establishes your ownership clearly.

Legal requirements for self-published books are minimal in most jurisdictions. You need to avoid plagiarism, respect trademark restrictions, and be honest in your marketing claims. If your book covers medical, legal, or financial advice, consider adding appropriate disclaimers.

Some countries require legal deposits of published books in national libraries. Others have requirements for books sold to residents. These requirements are usually automatic when you use major publishing platforms, but they're worth understanding if you're targeting international markets.

Tax implications vary by location and business structure. In the U.S., book royalties are generally treated as self-employment income. Keep records of your publishing expenses and consider consulting with an accountant if your book income becomes substantial.

Cover Design and Interior Formatting

Your cover sells your book before anyone reads a single word. This isn't negotiable or optional. An amateur cover will kill sales faster than bad reviews, unclear descriptions, or high prices.

Professional cover design costs $300 to $1,500 depending on complexity and designer experience. Pre-made covers cost $50 to $300 and work well if you can find one that fits your content and genre. DIY covers almost always look amateur unless you have genuine design skills.

Cover design isn't about personal preference or artistic expression. It's about marketing communication. Your cover needs to signal genre, quality level, and target audience instantly. It needs to look good as a thumbnail image in online stores. It needs to stand out among dozens of similar books.

Interior formatting is less visible but equally important for reader experience. Poor formatting makes books hard to read and reflects badly on your professionalism. Proper margins, readable fonts, consistent spacing, and logical chapter breaks are non-negotiable.

> ▲ Caution: Don't use your blog's fonts and formatting in your book. Screen reading and print reading have different requirements.

Amazon provides free formatting tools that handle most basic needs. Vellum (Mac only) creates professional-looking interiors with minimal effort. Reedsy Design Editor works in any browser and produces solid results. Professional formatters charge $200 to $800 but handle complex layouts and multiple formats.

Typography matters more than most authors realize. Your font choice affects readability, perceived quality, and reader fatigue. Stick with proven book fonts like Garamond, Minion, or Sabon for body text. Save decorative fonts for chapter headings and special elements.

Test your formatting on different devices and in different formats before publishing. What looks perfect on your computer screen might be unreadable on a phone or e-reader. Print a proof copy and read it carefully before approving the final version.

Distribution and Launch Strategy

Leveraging Your Existing Blog Audience

Here's your secret weapon: you already have people who know and trust your work. Most authors start from zero, begging strangers to care about their book. You get to skip that painful phase and go straight to people who are already invested in your success.

But don't assume your blog readers will buy your book automatically. They've been getting your content for free, and now you're asking them to pay for it. You need to make a compelling case for why the book offers value beyond what they're already getting from your blog.

Start talking about your book project months before it's finished. Share behind-the-scenes glimpses of your writing process. Ask for input on cover designs or chapter titles. Let your audience feel like they're part of the creation process, not just passive consumers of the final product.

> ★ Pro Tip: Create a simple landing page to collect email addresses from people interested in your book. Start building your launch list while you're still writing.

The biggest mistake bloggers make is treating their book like just another blog post. "Hey everyone, I wrote a book, here's the link." That's not a launch strategy, that's an afterthought. Your book deserves more fanfare than your average Tuesday post about productivity tips.

Create anticipation with a series of posts that preview the book's content without giving everything away. Share the story of why you decided to write it. Explain what readers will be able to do after reading it that they can't do now. Make people excited about the transformation your book promises.

Don't just announce the book once and move on. Plan multiple touchpoints over several weeks. Different people check your blog at different times, and even regular readers might miss a single announcement. Repetition isn't annoying if you're providing value each time.

Your most loyal blog readers can become your book's earliest advocates. They'll write the first reviews, share the announcement with their networks, and provide social proof that helps convince strangers to take a chance on your work.

Cross-Platform Promotion: Newsletter, Social, Podcast

Your blog is just one channel in your content mix. If you've been smart about building your audience, you have multiple ways to reach the same people and several opportunities to amplify your book launch.

Email newsletters have the highest conversion rates of any marketing channel. Newsletter subscribers are more engaged than social media followers and more likely to buy things you recommend. If you don't have a newsletter yet, start one immediately. If you do have one, treat your book launch like the most important campaign you've ever sent.

Social media works differently for book promotion than it does for regular content sharing. People scroll through social feeds quickly and need to see something multiple times before it registers. Plan a sustained campaign across several weeks, not a single announcement post.

> ▲ Caution: Don't turn every social media post into a book advertisement. Mix promotional content with your usual valuable posts to avoid alienating your audience.

LinkedIn works well for business books, Twitter for thought leadership topics, and Instagram for visual or lifestyle content. Tailor your messaging to each platform's audience and format requirements. A LinkedIn post about professional development will be different from an Instagram story about the same topic.

If you have a podcast, your book launch is perfect content for multiple episodes. You can discuss individual chapters, share stories from the writing process, interview other authors about their experiences, or answer listener questions about your book's topic.

Cross-promotion works both ways. Your book can drive people to your other content channels, and your other channels can drive people to your book. Include links to your newsletter, social accounts, and blog in your book. Mention your book in your newsletter signature and social media bios.

The goal isn't to spam people across every channel you have. It's to reach people where they're most likely to engage and give them multiple opportunities to discover your book without being obnoxious about it.

Amazon Optimization and Category Strategy

Amazon is a search engine that happens to sell books. People searching for solutions to problems you address in your book are potential customers, but only if they can find you among the millions of other options.

Your book's title, subtitle, and description are your primary SEO tools. Include keywords that people search for, not just clever phrases that sound good to you. "The Ultimate Guide to Freelance Writing Success" will be found more easily than "Words for Hire: My Journey Through the Gig Economy."

Categories matter more than most authors realize. Amazon lets you choose two categories, and picking the right ones can mean the difference between ranking on page one and disappearing into obscurity. Don't go for the most popular categories where you'll be competing against bestsellers. Find smaller, more targeted categories where you can rank.

> ■ Danger Zone: Don't choose categories based on where you think your book belongs. Choose based on where you can realistically compete and where your target readers browse.

Study the top books in your potential categories. Look at their titles, covers, descriptions, and pricing. You're not trying to copy them, but you need to understand what's working in your space. If all the top books in a category are priced at $9.99, your $2.99 book might seem cheap instead of attractively priced.

Keywords in your book description help with discoverability, but don't stuff them in unnaturally. Write for humans first, search engines second. Your description needs to convince people to buy, not just help them find you.

Reviews are the social proof that converts browsers into buyers. Amazon's algorithm favors books with more reviews, and customers trust books that other people have validated. Getting your first ten reviews is crucial for building momentum.

Launch timing can affect your ability to rank in categories and gain visibility. New releases get a temporary boost in Amazon's algorithm, but only if they generate sales quickly. Plan your launch for when you can drive the most traffic, not just when your book happens to be ready.

Pricing and Promotional Tactics

Pricing strategy for books is part psychology, part economics, and part guesswork. The right price depends on your goals, your audience, and your competition, but there are some principles that apply across most situations.

Higher prices can signal higher quality, but they also create more resistance to purchase. Lower prices remove barriers but might make your book seem less valuable. The sweet spot for most business books is $9.99 to $14.99 for ebooks and $12.99 to $19.99 for paperbacks.

Launch pricing often differs from long-term pricing. You might start with a lower introductory price to generate initial sales and reviews, then raise the price once you've established some momentum. Amazon allows you to change prices anytime, so you can experiment to find what works.

> ★ Pro Tip: Track your sales data closely during the first few weeks to see how price changes affect both unit sales and total revenue. Sometimes selling fewer books at higher prices is more profitable than high-volume, low-price sales.

Free promotions can jumpstart visibility but should be used strategically. Giving away your book for a few days can help you gain reviews and reach new readers, but it can also devalue your work and attract people who aren't serious about your topic.

Countdown deals and limited-time discounts create urgency without permanently lowering your book's perceived value. "Get it for $4.99 this week only" works better than just pricing it at $4.99 indefinitely.

Bundle strategies can increase average order value and provide more value to customers. If you have multiple books, offer them as a package. If you have courses or other products, use your book as an entry point to higher-value offerings.

The goal isn't to maximize revenue from book sales alone. Books are often loss leaders that introduce people to your other work, build your email list, or establish your credibility for speaking and consulting opportunities. Price accordingly based on your broader business objectives, not just immediate book profits.

Part III: Use Cases and Applications

Business and Professional Content

"The hardest part about writing a business book isn't explaining what you know. It's convincing people that what you know is worth paying for when they've been getting your advice for free on your blog." - Consultant turned author

---

Converting Industry Expertise into Authority

You've been writing about your industry for years, sharing insights, analyzing trends, and offering advice to anyone who stumbles across your blog. Now you want to package that expertise into something that positions you as the go-to authority in your field. The challenge is making your book feel definitive instead of derivative.

Industry expertise books work best when they solve problems that other resources ignore or handle poorly. Maybe the existing books in your field are written by academics who understand theory but not practice. Maybe they're written by consultants who work with Fortune 500 companies but don't understand small business realities. Maybe they're just outdated and don't reflect how your industry has changed in the past five years.

Your blog posts probably reveal gaps in existing resources through the questions your readers ask and the problems they can't solve elsewhere. These gaps are your book's opportunity. You're not trying to cover everything about your industry, you're trying to be the best resource for the things other people get wrong or ignore completely.

> ▲ Caution: Don't try to write the comprehensive guide to your entire industry. Focus on the subset where you have unique insights or superior approaches.

Authority comes from being narrow, not broad. "Marketing for B2B SaaS companies with 10-50 employees" is more authoritative than "Digital Marketing Strategies." "Managing remote development teams in fintech startups" beats "Leadership in Technology Companies." The narrower your focus, the easier it is to be the obvious expert choice.

Your existing blog content probably covers multiple aspects of your industry, but your book should follow a single thread that leads readers from their current state to their desired outcome. Maybe that thread is "How to transition from employee to consultant in accounting firms" or "Building a content marketing system that generates leads for manufacturing companies."

Case Study: Consultant Blog to Business Book

Let's look at how Priya Krishnamurthy turned her cybersecurity consulting blog into a book that landed her speaking gigs at major conferences and consulting contracts with Fortune 500 companies.

Priya had been blogging about cybersecurity for three years, covering everything from password policies to advanced threat detection. Her posts were technical and thorough, but scattered across dozens of topics. Her audience included IT professionals, security specialists, and business leaders who needed to understand cyber risks.

The breakthrough came when she analyzed her most popular posts and realized they all addressed the same underlying problem: the communication gap between technical security teams and business executives. Technical people couldn't explain risks in business terms, and executives couldn't make informed decisions about security investments.

Instead of trying to write a comprehensive cybersecurity guide, Priya focused her book on bridging this communication gap. She organized her existing content around a framework she called "Security ROI Translation" and wrote new material that showed both technical and business audiences how to speak each other's language.

> ★ Pro Tip: Look for the common thread that connects your most successful blog posts. That thread often reveals your unique angle for a book.

The book's structure followed a business decision-making process instead of a technical implementation sequence. Each chapter addressed a different stage: identifying risks, quantifying potential losses, evaluating solutions, building business cases for security investments, and measuring results. Her technical blog content was reframed to serve this business-focused narrative.

Priya's blog had established her credibility with technical audiences, but the book positioned her as someone who could speak to C-level executives. Within six months of publication, she was keynoting security conferences and consulting with companies that needed someone who could translate between technical and business teams.

The key was recognizing that her unique value wasn't just security expertise (plenty of people had that) but the ability to make security decisions accessible to non-technical decision makers. Her book became the definitive guide to that challenge.

B2B Content Adaptation Strategies

B2B blog content faces different challenges when converted to book format than B2C content does. Business readers are often looking for systems they can implement, frameworks they can adapt, and strategies they can present to their teams or bosses. They want practical content that produces measurable results.

Your blog posts might focus on individual tactics or problems, but your book needs to show how everything fits together into a comprehensive approach. B2B readers don't just want to know how to optimize their email subject lines, they want to understand how email optimization fits into their overall lead generation strategy.

Case studies and examples need to be more detailed and realistic in books than in blog posts. A blog post might mention that "Company X increased conversion rates by 40% using this technique." A book needs to explain Company X's starting point, the steps they took, the obstacles they encountered, and how readers can adapt the approach to their own situations.

■ Danger Zone: Don't include case studies without permission from the companies involved. Anonymize details or create composite examples based on multiple real situations.

B2B books also need to address implementation challenges that blog posts can skip. Who needs to be involved in making changes? How do you get buy-in from stakeholders? What resources are required? How do you measure success? Blog readers might figure out these details themselves, but book buyers expect more comprehensive guidance.

The language and tone for B2B books can be more professional than typical blog content, but don't sacrifice personality entirely. Business readers still want to connect with the author as a person, not just consume information from a corporate entity. Your expertise matters, but so does your perspective and approach.

Consider including templates, worksheets, and other practical tools that readers can use immediately. These resources add value that goes beyond the information in your blog posts and give readers tangible materials they can share with their teams.

Building Thought Leadership Through Publishing

A well-positioned business book doesn't just share information, it shapes how people think about your industry or functional area. Thought leadership means being the person others quote, reference, and turn to when they need expert perspective on your topic.

Your blog establishes your expertise, but your book establishes your framework. Blog posts can present individual ideas, but books can introduce new ways of thinking about familiar problems. Maybe you've identified patterns that others haven't noticed, or developed approaches that challenge conventional wisdom.

Thought leadership books often introduce new terminology or reframe existing concepts in more useful ways. If your blog has been developing ideas that don't have good names yet, your book is the opportunity to define them clearly and give them memorable labels that others will adopt.

The goal isn't just to be right about your topic, but to be influential in how others approach it. This means your book needs to be quotable, shareable, and memorable. Business readers should finish your book with new language for discussing familiar challenges and new frameworks for solving persistent problems.

> ★ Pro Tip: Include a glossary or index of your key concepts and frameworks. This makes your book more useful as a reference and increases the likelihood that others will cite your ideas.

Thought leadership also requires taking positions that others might disagree with. Safe, consensus opinions don't create thought leadership. Your book should challenge something that most people in your industry accept without question, or propose solutions that others haven't considered.

The authority you build through thought leadership extends far beyond book sales. It leads to speaking opportunities, media interviews, consulting engagements, and partnership opportunities that can be far more valuable than the direct revenue from your book.

But thought leadership requires consistency and follow-through. Your book is just the beginning of a longer conversation with your industry. You need to continue developing and refining your ideas through additional content, speaking engagements, and ongoing engagement with the community you're trying to influence.

Personal Brand and Lifestyle Content

"The difference between a personal blog and a personal brand book is the difference between a diary and a documentary. Both tell your story, but only one is designed for an audience." - Lifestyle blogger turned bestselling author

---

From Personal Blog to Memoir/Advice Book

Personal blogs are messy, meandering things. You write about your weekend adventures, your struggles with work-life balance, your opinions about everything from coffee shops to career changes. It's authentic and relatable, but it's not book material automatically.

The challenge with personal content is finding the universal themes buried in your individual experiences. Your readers don't care about your life because it's your life. They care because your experiences reflect their own struggles, aspirations, or curiosities. Your job is to extract the broadly applicable insights from your personal stories.

Start by identifying the transformation you've undergone that your blog has documented. Maybe you've gone from corporate employee to successful freelancer. Maybe you've navigated a major life change like divorce, parenthood, or career pivot. Maybe you've overcome a challenge that many people face but few talk about openly.

> ★ Pro Tip: The strongest personal brand books focus on one major transformation or life theme, not a collection of unrelated experiences and observations.

Your blog posts probably contain dozens of mini-stories and small revelations, but your book needs a coherent narrative arc that ties everything together. What was your starting point?

What obstacles did you face? What did you learn along the way? How did you change, and what can others learn from your journey?

The memoir elements provide the story, but the advice elements provide the value. Readers want to be entertained by your experiences, but they also want to benefit from your hard-won wisdom. Balance personal anecdotes with practical insights that readers can apply to their own situations.

Don't assume that interesting means important automatically. That hilarious story about your disastrous vacation might be perfect for your blog, but if it doesn't serve your book's larger purpose, it doesn't belong. Be ruthless about cutting content that doesn't advance your central narrative or provide value to readers.

Case Study: Travel Blog to Travel Guide

Marcus Hendricks had been blogging about budget travel for four years when he decided to write a book. His blog, "Broke but Not Broken," documented his adventures traveling through Southeast Asia, Eastern Europe, and Central America on less than $30 a day.

The blog was popular because Marcus was honest about the downsides of budget travel. He wrote about food poisoning in Thailand, getting ripped off in Prague, and sleeping in questionable hostels across three continents. His posts were funny, self-deprecating, and refreshingly realistic about the gap between Instagram travel photos and real travel experiences.

But when Marcus started organizing his blog content for a book, he realized he had a problem. His posts were entertaining stories, but they didn't provide systematic guidance for other budget travelers. He had plenty of cautionary tales but no clear framework for avoiding the mistakes he'd made.

> ▲ Caution: Don't assume that entertaining content translates to helpful content automatically. Personal stories need to serve a larger purpose in a book format.

Marcus solved this by restructuring his approach entirely. Instead of organizing the book chronologically around his travels, he organized it around the problems budget travelers face: planning routes, finding cheap accommodation, eating safely on a tight budget, avoiding scams, and dealing with emergencies abroad.

Each chapter combined his personal experiences with practical advice. The story about getting food poisoning became part of a chapter on eating safely while traveling. The tale of being overcharged for a taxi became part of a section on transportation scams. His blog content provided the entertaining examples, but the book provided the systematic guidance.

The result was "The $30 Traveler: How to See the World Without Going Broke," which became a bestseller in the travel category. Marcus had transformed his personal travel diary into a comprehensive guide that helped thousands of other travelers avoid his mistakes and replicate his successes.

The key was recognizing that his unique value wasn't just his travel experiences (lots of people travel on a budget) but his willingness to be honest about the challenges and his systematic approach to solving them.

Monetizing Personal Experience and Insights

Personal brand books can be harder to monetize directly than business books because the audience is often broader and less targeted. A book about freelance writing appeals to people who want to make money freelance writing. A book about your quarter-life crisis appeals to people who are interested in quarter-life crises, but that doesn't translate to purchasing behavior necessarily.

The monetization often comes from what the book enables instead of what it sells directly. Personal brand books can establish you as a speaker, coach, or consultant. They can open doors to media opportunities, partnership deals, or brand sponsorships. They can build an audience for other products or services you want to offer.

Think about what business you want to be in beyond writing books. Do you want to offer coaching or consulting services? Do you want to create courses or workshops? Do you want to become a paid speaker? Your book should position you for these opportunities while providing value to readers who just want to read your story.

> ■ Danger Zone: Don't write a personal brand book that's just therapy disguised as advice. If your primary motivation is processing your own experiences, see a therapist instead of writing a book.

Personal brand books also work well as lead magnets for higher-value offerings. If you're building a coaching business around life transitions, a book about your own transition can attract potential clients. If you're developing courses about pursuing unconventional careers, a book about your career journey can build credibility and audience.

The key is being clear about what transformation you're helping others achieve, not just what transformation you've experienced yourself. Your story is the vehicle, but their improvement is the destination.

Building Community Through Shared Stories

Personal brand books have unique power to create community among readers who share similar experiences or aspirations. When people read about your struggles with work-life balance, career changes, or life transitions, they often think "Finally, someone who gets it."

This community-building aspect can be more valuable than direct book sales. Readers who connect with your story become followers of your broader work. They join your email list, follow you on social media, attend your events, and recommend you to others facing similar challenges.

Your blog probably already has this community-building effect on a smaller scale. People comment on posts about their own similar experiences. They share your content with friends going through comparable situations. They return to your blog when they need encouragement or guidance.

A book amplifies this effect because it provides a more substantial shared experience. Someone who reads your entire book has invested hours in your story and perspective. They're more likely to feel connected to you and to other readers who have had the same experience.

> ★ Pro Tip: Include ways for readers to connect with each other, not just with you. This might be through social media hashtags, online communities, or local meetup groups.

Consider building community features around your book launch. Create Facebook groups for readers to discuss the book and share their own stories. Organize virtual or in-person events where people can meet others who are going through similar experiences. Encourage readers to share their own stories and insights.

The goal is to position yourself as the catalyst for a community, not just the center of attention. People want to connect with others who understand their challenges and aspirations. Your book can be the starting point for these connections, but the community should be able to thrive with or without your constant involvement.

This community-building approach also provides content and insights for future books, courses, or other offerings. When you understand what your readers are struggling with and what questions they're asking, you can develop products and services that serve their evolving needs.

The strongest personal brand books don't just tell your story, they invite readers into a larger conversation about the themes and challenges your story represents. They create a sense of belonging among people who might otherwise feel isolated in their experiences.

Educational and How-To Content

"The difference between a tutorial blog post and an educational book is like the difference between giving someone a fish and teaching them to become a fisherman. Both feed people, but only one builds lasting skills." - Programming instructor turned technical author

Tutorial Posts to Comprehensive Guides

Your how-to blog posts solve immediate problems for people who need quick answers. Someone searches "how to set up Google Analytics," finds your post, follows your steps, and moves on with their day. That's valuable, but it's not book-worthy on its own.

Educational books need to go deeper than individual tutorials. They need to teach underlying principles, explain why certain approaches work better than others, and help readers develop judgment about when to apply different techniques. Your blog post might show someone how to write a press release, but your book should teach them how to think like a publicist.

The challenge is organizing dozens of tactical posts into a learning progression that makes sense for someone starting from zero. Your blog readers might jump around based on their immediate needs, but book readers expect a logical sequence that builds knowledge systematically.

Start by identifying the skill or knowledge area that connects your best tutorial content. Maybe you've written fifty posts about different aspects of content marketing, from keyword research to email automation. Your book isn't just a collection of those tutorials, it's a complete system for mastering content marketing from beginner to advanced practitioner.

> ▲ Caution: Don't assume that more tutorials make a better educational book automatically. Focus on the most important techniques and explain them thoroughly instead of covering everything superficially.

Educational books also need to address the context that individual tutorials can skip. Why is this skill important? How does it fit into larger goals? What are the common mistakes beginners make? What should readers focus on first versus what can wait until they're more experienced?

Your tutorial posts probably assume readers have certain basic knowledge or tools. Books need to start from the true beginning and explain foundational concepts that might seem obvious to you. The person reading your book about social media marketing might not know what a hashtag is or how to create a business account on Instagram.

Case Study: Tech Blog to Programming Manual

Elena Vasquez had been blogging about web development for five years when she decided to write a book about building APIs with Node.js. Her blog, "Code Coffee," had hundreds of posts covering everything from basic JavaScript concepts to advanced backend architecture.

Her most popular posts were step-by-step tutorials that showed developers how to solve problems: "How to authenticate users with JWT tokens," "Building a RESTful API in 30 minutes," "Connecting your app to MongoDB." These posts got thousands of views and generated lots of engagement from developers who needed quick solutions.

But when Elena started outlining her book, she realized that her individual tutorials didn't add up to a coherent learning experience. Someone could follow her JWT authentication tutorial perfectly but still not understand how authentication fits into overall application security. They could build a basic API but not know how to scale it for production use.

Elena restructured her approach around the complete journey of building a real-world application. Instead of organizing chapters around individual techniques, she organized them around the stages of development: planning and design, setting up the development environment, building core functionality, adding authentication and security, optimizing performance, and deploying to production.

> ★ Pro Tip: Organize educational books around projects or outcomes, not just techniques. Readers learn better when they're working toward a concrete goal.

Each chapter combined multiple techniques from her blog posts but presented them in the context of building something complete. The authentication chapter didn't just show how to implement JWT tokens, it explained when to use different authentication strategies, how to handle edge cases, and how authentication decisions affect the rest of the application.

The book also included material that would never work in blog posts: detailed explanations of underlying concepts, comprehensive error handling strategies, and troubleshooting guides for common problems. Blog readers want quick answers, but book readers are willing to invest time in deeper understanding.

"Full-Stack APIs: Building Production-Ready Applications with Node.js" became a bestseller in the programming category and established Elena as a recognized expert in backend development. The book's success led to speaking opportunities, consulting contracts, and eventually her own online course platform.

Creating Workbook and Resource Elements

Educational books become more valuable when they include practical elements that readers can use to apply what they're learning. These might be worksheets, templates, checklists, or exercises that help readers practice new skills and track their progress.

Your blog posts might mention these resources in passing ("make sure to document your process" or "create a checklist for this workflow"), but books can include the tools themselves. Readers appreciate having everything they need in one place instead of having to create their own materials or search for resources elsewhere.

Workbook elements also help readers engage more actively with your content. Instead of just reading about how to create a content calendar, they can fill out a template you provide. Instead of just understanding the concept of customer personas, they can complete exercises that help them develop personas for their own business.

■ Danger Zone: Don't include worksheets or templates just for the sake of having them. Every resource should serve a clear purpose in helping readers achieve the book's learning objectives.

Consider what materials you wished you had when you were learning the skills your book teaches. What templates would have saved you time? What checklists would have helped you avoid mistakes? What exercises would have helped you practice new concepts?

These resources also extend the life and value of your book. Readers are more likely to keep books they can reference and use repeatedly. A book with useful templates becomes a permanent resource instead of something they read once and forget.

Digital resources work well for educational content. You can include links to downloadable templates, online tools, or updated resources that won't become outdated as quickly as printed materials. Just make sure the book remains valuable even if the digital resources become unavailable.

Updating Technical Content for Longevity

Technical and educational content faces a unique challenge: it becomes outdated faster than other types of content. Your blog post about setting up Facebook ads from 2019 might be completely irrelevant by 2024 because the platform has changed so dramatically.

When converting technical blog content to book format, focus on principles and approaches that are likely to remain relevant even as tools and platforms evolve. Instead of showing exactly which buttons to click in a software interface, teach the underlying logic of what readers are trying to accomplish.

Your book should help readers understand not just how to do something, but why it works and how to adapt when circumstances change. The steps for setting up Google Analytics might change, but the principles of tracking user behavior and measuring website performance will remain relevant.

Include version information and update dates for any technical instructions you do include. Be explicit about what might change and how readers can find current information when they need it. Point them to official documentation, community resources, or your own website where you can provide updates.

★ Pro Tip: Create a companion website or resource page for your book where you can post updates, corrections, and new information as tools and platforms evolve.

Consider writing your technical content at a slightly higher level of abstraction than your blog posts. Instead of "Click the blue button in the top right corner," write "Access the settings menu (usually located in the top navigation area)." This approach makes your instructions more durable and helps readers develop problem-solving skills.

Focus on teaching readers how to learn and adapt instead of just how to follow instructions. Show them how to find documentation, how to troubleshoot common problems, and how to stay current with changes in their field. These meta-skills are more valuable than any technical knowledge.

The goal isn't to create content that never needs updating, but to create content that degrades gracefully and remains useful even when some details become outdated. Readers should be able to apply your core concepts even if the tools and interfaces you mention have changed.

Educational books that teach timeless principles while acknowledging the reality of technical change serve readers better than books that try to be comprehensive references for rapidly evolving tools and platforms.

Creative and Artistic Content

"The hardest part about turning creative blog content into a book isn't the writing or the design. It's convincing yourself that your art is worth someone else's money." - Visual artist who spent three years procrastinating on her first book

Fiction Blogs to Published Novels

Fiction bloggers occupy a weird space in the content world. You're not solving problems or teaching skills like business bloggers. You're not documenting personal experiences like lifestyle bloggers. You're creating worlds, characters, and stories that exist purely for the joy of reading them.

This presents unique challenges when converting blog content to book format. Your serial fiction might have been perfect for weekly blog posts but feel choppy when read as a complete novel. Your short stories might be individually brilliant but lack the connective tissue needed for a cohesive collection.

The biggest mistake fiction bloggers make is assuming that published blog content equals ready-to-publish book content. Blog fiction is written for a different reading experience than novel fiction. Blog readers expect cliffhangers, shorter chapters, and more frequent payoffs. Book readers are willing to invest in longer character development and more complex plotting.

> ★ Pro Tip: Read your entire blog fiction from start to finish before making any publishing decisions. You'll discover pacing problems, continuity errors, and tonal inconsistencies that weren't obvious when you were posting weekly installments.

If you've been writing serial fiction on your blog, you probably need to do substantial revision work to make it function as a novel. Plot threads that worked when spread across months of posts might feel rushed or underdeveloped when read continuously. Characters who evolved naturally during your blogging might seem inconsistent when their entire arc is visible at once.

The revision process for blog-to-book fiction is often more intensive than starting from scratch. You're not just editing for grammar and style, you're restructuring narrative flow for a completely different reading experience. Some bloggers find it easier to use their blog fiction as source material for a new novel instead of trying to directly convert existing posts.

Consider your audience carefully too. Your blog readers chose to follow your fiction week by week because they enjoyed the serialized experience. Book buyers are making a different commitment and might have different expectations about genre, length, and storytelling style.

Poetry and Creative Writing Collections

Poetry blogs face the opposite problem from fiction blogs. Instead of having too much interconnected content, you probably have hundreds of individual poems with no obvious organizing principle beyond "I wrote these and posted them online."

The challenge is finding the thematic threads that can turn a collection of blog posts into a cohesive book. Maybe your poems written during a period share emotional themes or stylistic approaches. Maybe poems about certain subjects work together to create a larger statement or exploration.

Don't just chronologically arrange your blog posts and call it a poetry collection. Readers expect poetry books to have some kind of organizing logic, whether that's thematic progression, emotional journey, or formal exploration. Your job is to find that logic in your existing work or create it through selection and arrangement.

> ▲ Caution: Resist the temptation to include every poem you've ever written just because you have enough for a book-length collection. Quality and coherence matter more than quantity.

Many successful poetry collections from blog content focus on a period or experience in the author's life. Maybe you wrote extensively about grief, relationships, parenthood, or career changes. These life experiences can provide the thematic unity that transforms random poems into a meaningful collection.

Consider writing new poems to fill gaps in your collection's narrative or thematic arc. If your blog poems about heartbreak are strong but don't include the resolution or growth that came later, write new material that completes the emotional journey.

The physical presentation of poetry books matters more than it does for most other genres. Spacing, typography, and page layout affect how readers experience your poems. Don't assume that your blog's formatting will translate well to book format.

Photography Blogs to Coffee Table Books

Photography blogs are inherently visual, creating both opportunities and challenges when converting to book format. Your images might be stunning on screen but require different technical specs for print publication. Your blog's casual mix of photos and commentary might not translate to the more formal structure expected in photography books.

Coffee table books are expensive to produce and occupy a luxury market segment. Readers expect high-quality printing, paper, and binding that showcase your photography at its best. This means higher upfront costs and potentially smaller profit margins than text-based books.

The selection and sequencing of images becomes crucial in book format. Your blog might feature your best photos mixed with casual snapshots and behind-the-scenes content. A photography book needs more rigorous curation and often tells a visual story that unfolds across pages.

> ■ Danger Zone: Don't underestimate the technical requirements and costs involved in high-quality photography book production. Research printing options thoroughly before committing to this format.

Consider what story your photographs tell when viewed together. Maybe your travel blog contains the foundation for a book about a region or culture. Maybe your nature photography documents environmental changes in your local area. Maybe your portrait work captures a particular community or time period.

Text plays a supporting role in photography books, but it still matters. Your blog posts might contain the seeds of compelling captions, introductory essays, or artist statements that provide context for your images. Don't ignore the written component entirely.

The market for photography books is smaller and more specialized than markets for text-based books. Success often depends on finding the right niche audience and marketing through galleries, art fairs, and photography communities instead of traditional book channels.

Maintaining Creative Integrity in Commercial Publishing

Here's the tension every creative blogger faces when considering book publication: you started blogging to share your art freely with people who appreciated it. Now you're thinking about packaging that same art as a commercial product. How do you maintain your creative integrity while also creating something people will buy?

The first step is being honest about your motivations. Are you writing a book because you have something important to say that requires book-length treatment? Or are you writing a book because having a published book seems like the next logical step in building your creative career?

Neither motivation is wrong, but they lead to different approaches. If you're driven by artistic vision, focus on creating the best possible expression of your ideas and worry about commercial considerations later. If you're driven by career goals, research what's working in your genre and adapt your content accordingly.

Your blog audience provides valuable feedback about what resonates, but don't let their preferences completely dictate your book's direction. Blog readers represent a subset of potential book buyers, and their tastes might not reflect broader market preferences.

★ Pro Tip: Create a clear artistic mission statement for your book before you start worrying about commercial concerns. This gives you something to return to when market pressures threaten to compromise your vision.

Commercial publishing requires compromises, but not every compromise undermines creative integrity. Working with editors, designers, and marketers can improve your work by forcing you to clarify your ideas and communicate more effectively with readers.

The key is knowing which elements of your creative vision are non-negotiable and which are flexible. Maybe your poetry's emotional honesty is essential but the poems included can be adjusted. Maybe your photography's artistic style is crucial but the book's organization can be modified for better market appeal.

Publishing a book doesn't end your creative path, it documents one stage of it. Your book represents your artistic vision at a moment, not your final statement as a creative person. You can maintain integrity by being true to who you are now while remaining open to growth and change in future work.

Creative books often have longer commercial lifespans than business or how-to books because they're less tied to trends and current events. A poetry collection or photography book that finds its audience can continue selling for years without becoming outdated. This longer timeline can justify taking more creative risks and prioritizing artistic vision over immediate commercial appeal.

Part IV: Advanced Strategies

Multi-Format Content Strategy

"Publishing one book is like planting one tree. Building a content mix is like growing a forest. Both have their place, but only one creates sustainable, long-term value." - Content strategist with seven books and counting

Creating Book Series from Blog Categories

Your blog probably covers more ground than any single book should attempt. Maybe you write about marketing, productivity, leadership, and entrepreneurship. Each of these topics could be its own book, and probably should be if you want to serve your readers well and build a sustainable publishing strategy.

The mistake most bloggers make is trying to cram everything they know into one comprehensive guide. "The Complete Guide to Building a Successful Business" sounds impressive, but readers would be better served by separate books on marketing, operations, leadership, and finance. Focused books are easier to write, easier to market, and more valuable to readers.

Look at your blog categories as potential book topics. If you have fifty posts about email marketing and forty posts about social media strategy, you might have two books instead of one confused mess about "digital marketing." If you've written extensively about both freelancing and agency management, those are different audiences with different needs.

Series books create multiple opportunities for the same reader to buy from you. Someone who loves your book about freelance writing might also want your book about client management. Someone who benefits from your productivity system might be interested in your time management techniques. Cross-selling becomes natural when your books address related but distinct problems.

The key is finding the right level of detail for each book. "Social Media Marketing" might be too broad, but "Instagram Marketing for Small Businesses" could be just right. "Leadership" is probably too general, but "Leading Remote Teams" gives you a focused angle that can be thoroughly covered in book length.

Series also allow you to test topics and see what resonates before committing to larger projects. Your first book might reveal which aspects of your expertise generate the most interest and demand. Use that feedback to guide your subsequent book topics.

Repurposing Book Content Back to Blog

The content flow doesn't just go from blog to book. Your book research and writing process generates new material that can feed back into your blog, newsletter, and other content channels. This creates a virtuous cycle where each format supports and enhances the others.

Your book's table of contents becomes a content calendar. Each chapter topic can be broken down into multiple blog posts that explore different aspects or provide examples. A chapter about email marketing might spawn posts about subject line optimization, automation workflows, and deliverability best practices.

The research you do for your book often uncovers interesting tangents that don't fit the book's scope but make perfect blog content. Maybe you interview experts for case studies but only use portions of those conversations in the book. The unused material becomes podcast episodes or blog posts.

> ★ Pro Tip: Keep a "blog ideas" file while writing your book. You'll constantly encounter topics that are related to your book but don't belong in it. Capture these ideas for future content.

Book writing also deepens your expertise in ways that improve all your content. The process of organizing your thoughts for book-length treatment often reveals connections and insights that wouldn't have emerged from writing individual blog posts. This enhanced understanding makes your subsequent blog content more sophisticated and valuable.

Don't just extract content from your book for blog posts. Use your book as a foundation for entirely new content that builds on the ideas you've developed. If your book establishes a framework or methodology, your blog posts can show how to apply it to situations you didn't have space to cover in the book.

Newsletter Integration and Cross-Promotion

Your newsletter is the perfect bridge between your blog and book content. Newsletter subscribers are your most engaged audience and most likely book buyers. They're also the people most interested in getting deeper insights and behind-the-scenes content about your book project.

Start talking about your book in your newsletter long before it's published. Share excerpts, discuss challenges you're facing in the writing process, and ask for input on covers or titles. This builds anticipation and makes subscribers feel invested in your book's success.

Your book launch should be a major newsletter event, not just a single announcement. Plan a series of emails that provide value while promoting the book. Maybe you share bonus content that didn't make it into the book, offer exclusive discounts to subscribers, or provide resources that complement the book's content.

The relationship works in reverse too. Your book can drive newsletter signups from readers who want to stay connected with your work. Include newsletter signup information in your book, offer exclusive content to newsletter subscribers who bought the book, and use your book's success to attract new subscribers.

> ■ Danger Zone: Don't turn your newsletter into a constant book promotion machine. Continue providing the regular value subscribers expect while strategically incorporating book-related content.

Newsletter content often provides the seeds for future books. Reader questions, popular topics, and engagement patterns reveal what your audience wants to learn more about. Use this feedback to identify gaps in your content that could become your next book project.

Consider creating newsletter-exclusive content that complements your book. Maybe you send monthly case studies that show how readers are applying your book's concepts. Maybe you provide updates and new developments in your field that keep your book's content current.

Building an Ecosystem of Related Products

Books rarely exist in isolation. They're often one component of a larger business strategy that might include courses, consulting, speaking, or software products. Your blog-to-book project can be the foundation for this broader ecosystem.

Your book establishes your credibility and expertise, but it's probably not your highest-value offering. A $15 book might lead to a $500 course, which might lead to a $5,000 consulting engagement. Think of your book as the entry point to a relationship, not the end goal.

Courses are a natural extension of book content. Your book might teach concepts and provide examples, while your course offers hands-on implementation support, templates, and community interaction. The book gives people enough information to understand the value of your approach, and the course gives them everything they need to implement it successfully.

Speaking opportunities often follow book publication. Conference organizers and event planners see published authors as more credible and promotable than bloggers. Your book becomes your speaker's credentials and provides ready-made presentation topics.

Consulting and coaching services can command much higher rates when you're a published author. Your book demonstrates your expertise and approach, making it easier for potential clients to understand what you offer and why they should hire you.

> ★ Pro Tip: Design your book with your broader business goals in mind. Include calls-to-action for your other services, but make sure they feel natural and valuable instead of promotional.

Software tools and apps can also extend your book's concepts into practical implementation. If your book teaches a productivity system, an app that helps people implement that system could be valuable. If your book covers marketing frameworks, templates and tools that make those frameworks easier to use create revenue opportunities.

The key is ensuring that each component of your ecosystem provides genuine value on its own while also supporting your other offerings. Your book should be worth reading even if someone never buys anything else from you. Your course should be valuable even if someone never hires you for consulting. This integrity builds trust and long-term relationships with your audience.

But don't try to build the entire ecosystem at once. Start with your book, see how it performs and what opportunities it creates, then gradually add complementary offerings based on what your audience wants and needs.

Technology and Automation

Tools for Content Extraction and Organization

Converting years of blog content into book format manually is like sorting your sock drawer one thread at a time. Technically possible, but there are better ways to spend your life. The right tools can turn months of tedious copy-pasting into hours of strategic content curation.

Start with something as simple as exporting your blog content into a format you can work with. WordPress, Medium, and most blogging platforms offer export functions that give you all your posts in XML or CSV format. This raw export won't be pretty, but it's better than manually copying each post.

Once you have your content exported, you need tools to organize and analyze it. Spreadsheet software becomes your best friend here. Import your post titles, publication dates, categories, and word counts into a spreadsheet where you can sort, filter, and identify patterns. You might discover that you've written 15,000 words about email marketing without realizing it.

★ Pro Tip: Use word count and engagement metrics to identify your strongest content. Posts that are both long and popular often contain the seeds of your best book chapters.

Text analysis tools can help you identify themes and topics across your content. Tools like Voyant or even simple word cloud generators can reveal which concepts you return to most frequently. This isn't a substitute for human judgment, but it can highlight patterns you might have missed.

For organizing content into book structure, outlining tools like Scrivener, Notion, or even Google Docs can help you group related posts and see how they might flow together. The key is getting all your content into a system where you can easily move pieces around and experiment with different organizational approaches.

Don't overlook simple automation scripts if you're technically inclined. A basic Python script can extract information from your blog exports, clean up formatting, or identify posts that meet certain criteria. Even simple find-and-replace operations can save hours of manual editing.

AI-Assisted Editing and Improvement

AI writing tools have gotten scary good at helping with the mechanical aspects of editing and revision. They're not going to write your book for you (and you wouldn't want them to), but they can handle a lot of the tedious cleanup work that turns blog posts into book chapters.

Grammar and style checkers like Grammarly or ProWritingAid can catch errors and inconsistencies across large volumes of text. When you're combining posts written months or years apart, these tools help identify places where your writing style has evolved or where you've been inconsistent with terminology.

AI-powered editing tools can also help with voice consistency. If your early blog posts were more formal and your recent ones are more conversational, AI can suggest revisions that bring everything into alignment with your current style. Just don't let the AI flatten your personality out of your writing entirely.

> ▲ Caution: Use AI editing suggestions as starting points, not final decisions. The tools are good at identifying potential problems but terrible at understanding context and intent.

Content summarization tools can help you identify the key points in long blog posts, making it easier to extract the essential information for your book. This is useful when you're condensing multiple posts into a single chapter and need to avoid redundancy.

AI can also help generate transition text between sections that weren't originally designed to flow together. Give it the ending of one blog post and the beginning of another, and ask it to suggest bridge paragraphs that connect the ideas smoothly.

Some AI tools can analyze your writing for readability and suggest ways to make complex ideas more accessible. This is valuable when converting expert-level blog content for a broader book audience.

But AI tools are supplements to human judgment, not replacements for it. They can speed up certain tasks and catch problems you might miss, but they can't understand your audience, your goals, or the nuances of your expertise the way you can.

Automated Formatting and Publishing Workflows

Once you've written your book, you need to get it formatted and published across multiple platforms. Doing this manually for each platform is mind-numbing work that's perfect for automation.

Pandoc is a powerful command-line tool that can convert your manuscript between different formats. Write in Markdown, and Pandoc can generate Word documents for editors, PDFs for print, ePub files for ebooks, and HTML for web publication. Learning Pandoc's syntax takes some effort, but it pays off when you need to make changes that propagate across all formats.

For simpler needs, tools like Reedsy Design Editor or Book Brush can automate much of the formatting process through web interfaces. You upload your text, choose a template, and get professionally formatted files for different publishing platforms.

> ■ Danger Zone: Don't get so caught up in automation that you lose control over the final output. Always review automated formatting carefully before publishing.

Publishing platforms themselves offer increasing automation. Amazon's KDP, Draft2Digital, and other services can convert your files to appropriate formats automatically and distribute them to multiple retailers. Set up your book once, and it appears on Amazon, Apple Books, Kobo, and other platforms simultaneously.

Metadata management becomes crucial when you're publishing across multiple platforms. Tools like ISBN databases and book cataloging systems help ensure your book information is consistent everywhere it appears. Inconsistent titles, descriptions, or author names can confuse readers and hurt discoverability.

Consider setting up automated social media posting for your book launch. Tools like Buffer or Hootsuite can schedule promotional posts across multiple platforms, announce milestones like hitting bestseller ranks, and share reader reviews as they come in.

Email automation can also support your book launch. Set up sequences that trigger when someone buys your book, thanking them for their purchase and offering resources. Create follow-up sequences that ask for reviews a few weeks after purchase.

Analytics and Performance Tracking

You can't improve what you don't measure, and book publishing generates a lot of data worth tracking. The key is identifying which metrics matter for your goals and setting up systems to monitor them consistently.

Sales data is obviously important, but it's not the only thing that matters. Track where your sales are coming from, which marketing efforts are driving purchases, and how your book's performance changes. Amazon's KDP dashboard provides detailed sales information, but you might want to export this data into spreadsheets for deeper analysis.

Review tracking helps you understand how readers are responding to your book. Set up Google Alerts for your book title and author name to catch reviews and mentions across the web. Monitor reviews on Amazon, Goodreads, and other platforms to identify common praise and complaints.

★ Pro Tip: Track both quantity and quality of reviews. A book with 50 four-star reviews often performs better than one with 10 five-star reviews.

Website analytics can show how your book is affecting traffic to your other content. Look for increases in blog readership, email signups, and engagement after your book launch. Your book should be driving people to your other content, not just generating direct sales.

Social media analytics can reveal which types of book-related content resonate with your audience. Track engagement on posts about your writing process, book excerpts, and promotional announcements. Use this data to refine your marketing approach for future books.

Email marketing metrics become important around book launches. Track open rates, click-through rates, and conversions for book-related emails. Test different subject lines, send times, and content approaches to optimize your email marketing.

Set up automated reporting systems that compile your key metrics into weekly or monthly summaries. This saves time and ensures you're regularly reviewing your book's performance instead of just checking sporadically.

Long-term tracking is often more valuable than short-term metrics. Your book's impact on your speaking opportunities, consulting inquiries, and overall business might not show up for months after publication. Keep notes on opportunities that arise from your book so you can measure its broader business impact.

The goal isn't to track everything possible, but to track the things that help you make better decisions about your current book's marketing and your future book projects. Use data to understand what's working, what isn't, and what you should do differently next time.

"The only thing worse than dealing with copyright law is dealing with tax law. The only thing worse than dealing with tax law is dealing with both at the same time while trying to figure out if your LLC can deduct that coffee you bought while writing." - Author's accountant, probably

---

Copyright and Republishing Rights

Here's the good news: you own the copyright to your blog posts automatically. The moment you hit "publish," that content is yours under copyright law in most countries. The potentially complicated news is that republishing your own content in a book isn't always as straightforward as it seems.

If you've been guest posting on other blogs or publications, you might have signed agreements that complicate your republishing rights. Some publications require exclusive rights to content, meaning you can't republish it elsewhere without permission. Others might have first publication rights or require attribution when you republish.

Check any contributor agreements you've signed before including guest post content in your book. Most blogging platforms and personal websites don't restrict your republishing rights, but corporate blogs, magazines, and professional publications often do. When in doubt, ask for permission rather than assuming you're in the clear.

★ Pro Tip: Keep a simple spreadsheet tracking where you've published content and what rights you've retained. This saves hours of detective work later when you're trying to remember what you can legally republish.

Your own blog content is generally safe to republish, but there are some edge cases to consider. If you've used images, quotes, or other content from third parties in your blog posts, make sure you have the rights to republish those elements in a commercial book. Fair use for blogs doesn't automatically extend to books.

The copyright page in your book should clearly state your ownership of the content and the year of first publication. If you're republishing content that was originally published across multiple years, you might need to list multiple copyright dates or choose the most recent year.

Consider registering your book's copyright with the U.S. Copyright Office if you're concerned about protection. This isn't required for copyright to exist, but it provides additional legal protections and makes it easier to pursue legal action if someone infringes your work.

When Blog Comments and Guest Posts Complicate Things

Blog comments create an interesting gray area when you're converting posts to book format. Technically, commenters own the copyright to their contributions, even if they're posted on your blog. You can't republish substantial portions of comments without permission.

Most blog-to-book conversions don't include comments anyway, so this isn't usually a practical problem. But if you want to include reader feedback, testimonials, or interesting discussions from your comment sections, you need to get permission from the commenters or paraphrase their contributions rather than quoting directly.

Guest posts on your blog create different complications. If you've published content by other authors on your blog, you can't include that content in your book without their explicit permission. This seems obvious, but it can be tricky when guest authors have contributed to collaborative posts or interview-style content.

> ▲ Caution: Don't assume that because someone posted content on your blog, you have the rights to republish it commercially. When in doubt, ask for written permission.

The safest approach is to only include content that you personally wrote for your book. If you want to include contributions from others, create clear agreements about how that content can be used. Get these agreements in writing, even if it's just an email exchange.

Some bloggers have created problems for themselves by promising guest authors that their content would only appear on the blog, then later wanting to include it in a book. Be transparent about your potential book plans when working with guest contributors.

If you do include content from others in your book, make sure you credit them appropriately and honor any agreements you made about attribution. This isn't just legally required, it's good professional practice that maintains relationships with your collaborators.

Business Structure for Publishing Income

Publishing income complicates your tax situation whether you earn $100 or $100,000 from your book. The question is whether the complexity is worth addressing through a formal business structure or if you can handle it as personal income.

Most beginning authors can treat book income as miscellaneous self-employment income on their personal tax returns. You'll pay income tax plus self-employment tax on your profits, and you can deduct legitimate business expenses like editing, cover design, and marketing costs.

As your publishing income grows, forming an LLC or other business entity might make sense for liability protection and tax advantages. An LLC can provide some protection for your personal assets if someone decides to sue you over your book content. It also allows for more sophisticated business expense tracking and potential tax benefits.

■ Danger Zone: Don't set up a complex business structure just because it sounds professional. The administrative overhead might not be worth it for small publishing income.

The decision often comes down to how serious you are about publishing as a business venture. If you're planning to publish multiple books, offer related services, or build a substantial content business, formal business structure makes more sense than if you're just testing the waters with one book.

Consider consulting with an accountant or attorney who understands publishing businesses before making major structural decisions. The right choice depends on your specific situation, income level, and long-term goals. What works for a full-time author might be overkill for someone publishing one book as a side project.

Different business structures have different tax implications, liability protections, and administrative requirements. Sole proprietorship is simplest but offers no liability protection. LLCs provide protection and flexibility but require more paperwork. Corporations offer the most protection but come with the most complexity.

Tax Implications and Record Keeping

Publishing income is subject to both income tax and self-employment tax in the United States, which can be a shock if you're not prepared for it. Self-employment tax alone is 15.3% of your net profit, on top of whatever income tax bracket you're in.

The good news is that you can deduct legitimate business expenses from your publishing income before calculating taxes. Editing costs, cover design, marketing expenses, software subscriptions, and even a portion of your home office can potentially be deducted if they're used for your publishing business.

Keep detailed records of all publishing-related income and expenses from day one. This includes royalty payments from

Amazon or other platforms, payments for professional services, software subscriptions, marketing costs, and any other money you spend on your book project.

> ★ Pro Tip: Set up a separate bank account for your publishing business, even if you're not forming a formal business entity. This makes tracking income and expenses much easier at tax time.

Save receipts and documentation for everything. The IRS might want to see proof that your cover design expense was legitimate or that your home office deduction is accurate. Digital receipts are fine, but make sure you have a system for organizing them.

Consider making quarterly estimated tax payments if your book generates significant income. The IRS expects you to pay taxes on self-employment income throughout the year, not just when you file your annual return. Underpayment penalties can be expensive if you owe a lot at tax time.

International sales can complicate your tax situation, especially if you're selling through platforms that operate in multiple countries. Different countries have different tax treaties with the United States, and you might need to file additional forms or pay taxes in multiple jurisdictions.

Book sales royalties are generally considered ordinary income, not capital gains, even if your book continues earning money for years after publication. This means you'll pay your regular income tax rate on royalties, not the potentially lower capital gains rate.

Keep records for at least three years after filing your tax return, longer if you're claiming substantial deductions or if your publishing business grows significantly. The IRS can audit returns up to three years after filing in most cases, six years if they suspect substantial underreporting of income.

The complexity of publishing taxes increases quickly as your income grows or if you expand into multiple revenue streams. What starts as simple self-employment income can become complicated when you add speaking fees, course sales, consulting income, and multiple book royalties. Plan for this complexity before it becomes overwhelming.

Part V: Execution Framework

The 90-Day Blog-to-Book System

Week-by-Week Implementation Plan

Most bloggers fail at the book conversion process not because they lack good content or writing ability, but because they treat it like an open-ended creative project instead of a business initiative with deadlines and deliverables. Ninety days gives you enough time to do quality work without so much time that you lose momentum or get distracted by other projects.

Weeks 1-2 are about foundation and assessment. Start by exporting all your blog content and getting it into a workable format. Create a spreadsheet with post titles, word counts, publication dates, and categories. This isn't creative work, it's data entry, but it's essential for everything that follows.

Analyze your content for themes and natural groupings. Print out summaries of your strongest posts and spread them on a table or wall where you can see patterns. You're looking for the story that connects your individual posts into something larger.

Write your one-sentence book description during week two. This forces you to clarify what your book is about and who it's for. Everything else you do in the next 88 days should support this central premise.

Weeks 3-4 focus on structure and planning. Create your detailed table of contents based on the content clusters you identified. Don't just organize your existing posts, arrange them into a logical learning progression that serves readers who haven't been following your blog for years.

Identify gaps where you need new content to bridge between existing posts or provide missing foundational information. Estimate how much new writing you'll need to do and block out time for it in your schedule.

★ Pro Tip: Plan to write 30-40% new content even if you think your existing posts are complete. The transitions, introductions, and context needed for book format always require more writing than you expect.

Weeks 5-8 are where you stop planning and start building. Copy your existing posts into your book structure and begin writing the connecting material that turns individual blog posts into cohesive chapters.

Don't edit for perfection during this phase. Your goal is to create a complete first draft that flows from beginning to end. Focus on making sure each chapter leads logically to the next and that you're not repeating yourself unnecessarily.

Read everything aloud as you go. Your ear will catch flow problems that your eye misses, and reading aloud forces you to experience your content the way readers will.

Weeks 9-10 are for major revision. Step away from your manuscript for a few days, then read it straight through as if you're encountering it for the first time. Mark sections that feel redundant, confusing, or off-topic. This is where you make the big structural changes that turn a collection of posts into a real book.

Be brutal about cutting content that doesn't serve your book's purpose. That clever tangent might be interesting, but if it doesn't help readers achieve the transformation your book promises, it doesn't belong.

Weeks 11-12 are for professional polish. Focus on sentence-level editing, fact-checking, and consistency. Verify that your examples are current, your statistics are accurate, and your advice reflects your current thinking instead of outdated approaches from old blog posts.

If you're working with a professional editor, this is when you send them your manuscript. If you're self-editing, take another break before doing your final review. Fresh eyes catch problems that familiarity obscures.

Common Roadblocks and Solutions

Perfectionism paralysis hits when you keep revising the first chapter instead of moving forward because it doesn't feel ready. The solution is to accept that first drafts are supposed to be imperfect. Set a timer for each chapter and move on when time is up, regardless of how polished it feels.

Scope creep happens when your book keeps growing as you think of more topics to include. You started with a focused idea about email marketing and now you're trying to cover all of digital marketing. The solution is returning to your one-sentence book description and ruthlessly cutting anything that doesn't support it.

Motivation loss usually strikes around week six when the initial excitement wears off and writing feels like drudgery. The solution is remembering that this is normal and pushing through the middle phase where most people quit. Focus on completing small daily tasks instead of thinking about the entire project.

⚠ Caution: Don't use research or planning as procrastination. If you find yourself constantly researching "the best way to structure a book" instead of structuring your book, you're avoiding the work.

Technical overwhelm happens when you get stuck on formatting, cover design, or publishing platform decisions instead of focusing on content. The solution is to make quick decisions about technical details and move forward. You can always change covers or reformat later, but you can't publish a book that doesn't exist.

Imposter syndrome kicks in when you start questioning whether you're qualified to write a book or whether anyone will want to read it. The solution is recognizing that your blog readers already validate your expertise. You're not inventing new credibility, you're packaging existing credibility in a new format.

Quality Control Checkpoints

Build quality control into your process instead of hoping to catch problems at the end. Schedule review points where you assess your progress and make corrections before moving forward.

Your week 4 checkpoint is structure review. Does your table of contents tell a compelling story? Can someone read the chapter titles and understand what transformation your book promises? If not, revise your structure before you start writing.

Week 8 is for flow assessment. Read your first draft straight through. Does each chapter lead naturally to the next? Are you repeating information unnecessarily? Do you contradict yourself anywhere? Fix major flow problems before moving to detailed editing.

Week 10 focuses on purpose alignment. Compare your finished first draft to your original one-sentence description. Does the book you wrote match the book you planned? If you've drifted from your original vision, decide whether to revise the book or update your description.

> ■ Danger Zone: Don't skip quality checkpoints because you're behind schedule. It's better to extend your timeline than to publish a book with fundamental structural problems.

Week 12 is your professional standards checkpoint. Does your book meet basic professional standards for grammar, formatting, and presentation? Would you be comfortable seeing this book in a bookstore next to traditionally published works? If not, invest in editing or formatting help.

Launch Preparation Timeline

Your book launch doesn't start when you hit "publish." It starts weeks before with preparation that determines whether your book finds its audience or disappears into the vast ocean of published content.

Six weeks before launch, focus on platform preparation. Set up your Amazon KDP account and any other publishing platforms you plan to use. Research categories, keywords, and pricing for similar books. Don't wait until your book is finished to figure out where and how you'll publish it.

Four weeks before launch, create your marketing assets. Design your cover, write your book description, and create any promotional materials you'll need. Set up landing pages for pre-orders if you're using platforms that support them.

> ★ Pro Tip: Start building your launch email roster as soon as you begin writing your book. The people most likely to buy your book are those who are interested enough to sign up for updates about your progress.

Two weeks before launch, focus on review collection. Send advance copies to people who might provide reviews or endorsements. This includes loyal blog readers, fellow authors in your niche, and anyone else whose opinion carries weight with your target audience.

One week before launch, do your final systems check. Upload your final files, double-check all your metadata, and verify that everything is working correctly. Schedule social media posts, prepare email announcements, and confirm any promotional activities you've planned.

Launch week is about execution and monitoring. Announce your book across all your platforms, monitor early sales and reviews, and be prepared to make quick adjustments if something isn't working. The first week often determines how much momentum your book builds.

The 90-day timeline isn't arbitrary. It's long enough to produce quality work but short enough to maintain focus and urgency. Longer timelines tend to result in projects that drag on indefinitely. Shorter timelines usually sacrifice quality for speed.

Completing your book in 90 days doesn't mean your work is finished. Marketing, promotion, and building on your book's success are ongoing activities that extend well beyond the publication date. But having a finished, published book changes everything about how you approach these activities.

"Success in publishing is like success in dating. Everyone has different definitions, most people lie about their numbers, and the ones who seem most confident are usually making it up as they go along." - Author who wishes she'd understood this sooner

---

Defining Success Metrics Beyond Sales

Sales numbers are the most obvious measure of book success, but they're not the only measure that matters. A book that sells 500 copies but generates $50,000 in speaking fees is more successful than a book that sells 5,000 copies and leads to nothing else. A book that builds your email roster by 2,000 engaged subscribers might be worth more than immediate royalty payments.

Your success metrics should align with your original goals for writing the book. If you wanted to establish credibility in your field, measure speaking invitations, media mentions, and consulting inquiries. If you wanted to build your audience, track email signups, social media followers, and blog traffic increases. If you wanted direct revenue, focus on sales numbers and profit margins.

Authority building shows up in ways that are harder to quantify but often more valuable than sales. Are people citing your book in articles or presentations? Are you being invited to participate in podcasts, panels, or expert roundups? Are potential clients mentioning your book when they reach out about services?

Lead generation effectiveness can be measured through tracking codes, special landing pages, or simply asking new contacts how they found you. If your book is working as intended, you should see increases in inquiries for your other products and services, not just book sales.

★ Pro Tip: Set up Google Alerts for your name and book title to track mentions and discussions you might otherwise miss. These informal metrics often reveal impact that doesn't show up in sales reports.

Brand building happens gradually and shows up in how people perceive and talk about your work. Are you being invited to larger, more prestigious opportunities? Are people introducing you differently at events? Has your book changed how others in your industry see your expertise?

Don't ignore negative metrics either. If your book generates sales but increases customer complaints about your other products, something is wrong with how you positioned your expertise. If speaking opportunities increase but audience engagement decreases, your book might be attracting the wrong type of attention.

Using Book Performance to Improve Blog Strategy

Your book's reception provides valuable feedback about what resonates with your audience and what doesn't. This intelligence should flow back into your blog strategy and help you create more effective content going forward.

Reader reviews often contain detailed feedback about which concepts were most helpful, which examples resonated, and which parts felt confusing or irrelevant. This feedback is gold for bloggers because it tells you exactly what topics and approaches your audience values most.

Sales data by chapter (if you publish on platforms that provide this information) or reader engagement with different sections can reveal which of your expertise areas have the strongest market demand. Maybe your chapter on productivity systems gets mentioned in every review, while your chapter on time management gets ignored.

▲ Caution: Don't assume that what works in book format will work in blog format automatically, or vice versa. The audiences and consumption patterns are different enough that you need to adapt your approach.

Book marketing that drives blog traffic can show you which promotional channels and messages are most effective for reaching your audience. If LinkedIn posts about your book generate more blog visitors than Twitter posts, that suggests where you should focus your ongoing content promotion efforts.

The questions readers ask about your book reveal gaps in your content that could become future blog posts. If multiple people ask for clarification about a concept you covered briefly in the book, that concept probably deserves a detailed blog post or series.

Use your book's table of contents as a content calendar for the months following publication. Each chapter can be broken down into multiple blog posts that explore related topics, provide examples, or address questions that readers have raised.

Planning Follow-Up Books and Series

Most successful authors don't stop at one book, and your first book's performance should inform decisions about future publishing projects. The data you gather from your first book makes subsequent books more likely to succeed because you better understand what your audience wants.

Topic validation happens naturally when you see which aspects of your first book generate the most interest and engagement. If readers consistently mention one chapter as valuable, that chapter's topic might be worth expanding into a full book.

Audience feedback often includes direct requests for follow-up content. Pay attention to comments like "I wish you'd covered X in more detail" or "Have you considered writing about Y?" These suggestions come from people who have already invested time and money in your content.

Series planning becomes easier once you understand how readers consume and respond to your work. Maybe your comprehensive guide approach worked well and you should continue with that format. Maybe readers preferred your tactical chapters over strategic ones, suggesting a more hands-on approach for future books.

> ■ Danger Zone: Don't rush into a second book just because your first one was successful. Take time to understand why it succeeded and whether you can replicate those conditions with different content.

Market positioning for subsequent books can build on the authority established by your first book. Your second book doesn't need to re-establish your credibility in the same way your first one did, giving you more freedom to explore related topics or take different approaches.

Consider the business environment you want to build around your content. If your first book drives consulting leads successfully, your second book might focus on a different aspect of the same problem. If your first book built a great email roster but didn't generate direct revenue, your second book might target a more targeted, higher-value audience.

Long-Term Content and Publishing Strategy

Think of your book as one component of a larger content strategy that spans multiple years and formats. Your blog, newsletter, speaking topics, course content, and future books should work together to build a comprehensive platform around your expertise.

Content repurposing becomes more sophisticated as you publish more books. A blog post might become a book chapter, then becomes a course module, then becomes a workshop presentation. Each format reaches different audiences and serves different purposes, but they all reinforce your core messages and expertise.

Platform building accelerates when you have multiple books supporting your broader content strategy. Each book introduces new readers to your work, and your blog keeps them engaged between publications. Your newsletter nurtures the relationship and promotes new releases. Speaking engagements showcase your expertise to audiences who might not have discovered your written content.

Revenue diversification often follows naturally from successful book publishing. Books establish credibility that leads to speaking fees, consulting contracts, course sales, and other opportunities. Your content strategy should account for these multiple revenue streams instead of depending solely on book sales or blog advertising.

> ★ Pro Tip: Create a master content calendar that shows how your blog posts, newsletter content, speaking topics, and book projects support each other throughout the year.

Authority amplification happens when consistent, high-quality content across multiple formats reinforces your reputation in your field. Your blog establishes your voice, your books demonstrate your depth of knowledge, and your speaking engagements show your ability to communicate with different audiences.

Long-term sustainability requires balancing content creation with other business activities. You can't just keep writing more books forever without considering how they fit into your broader career goals and business strategy.

The most successful content creators treat their publishing activities as investments in long-term platform building instead of just attempts to generate immediate revenue. Each piece of content, whether it's a blog post or a book, should move you closer to your larger goals of influence, authority, and business success.

Your first book is just the beginning of this journey. The lessons you learn from converting blog content to book format, from marketing your first publication, and from building an audience around your ideas will inform everything you do afterward. Use these lessons wisely, and your content strategy will compound in value during the years to come.

"Social media for authors is like dating: everyone has advice, most of it's terrible, and the people who seem most confident are usually making it up as they go along." - Marketing consultant who finally figured out the difference between engagement and actual sales

---

You know social media matters for book marketing. Everyone tells you to "build your platform" and "engage your audience." What they don't tell you is exactly how to post, what to say, or which hashtags won't make you look like a desperate amateur trying to game the system.

This chapter gets tactical. Real platform strategies, actual post formats that work, hashtag research that doesn't involve throwing spaghetti at the wall, and content planning that doesn't require hiring a social media manager or spending your life glued to your phone.

The fundamentals stay consistent across platforms: provide value, be authentic, engage genuinely. The execution details change constantly. Master the principles, adapt the tactics, and remember that social media starts conversations, not closes them.

Platform-Specific Strategies That Work

LinkedIn operates on professional credibility and industry insights. Your posts should position you as someone worth knowing in your field, not someone desperately trying to sell books. Share behind-the-scenes glimpses of your writing process, industry observations that demonstrate your expertise, and stories that humanize your professional experience.

The LinkedIn algorithm favors posts that generate meaningful comments over likes or shares. Ask questions that require thoughtful answers. Share controversial but defensible opinions about your industry. Post about failures and lessons learned, not just successes and achievements.

LinkedIn post structure that works: Hook in the first line, story or insight in the middle, call-to-action or question at the end. Keep paragraphs short and use line breaks generously. People scroll quickly and need visual breathing room.

Twitter thrives on personality and quick insights. Your thread about the three mistakes that kill most content marketing campaigns will get more engagement than your announcement that you wrote a book about content marketing. Save the direct promotion for when you've earned attention through valuable content.

Twitter threads work better than single tweets for complex ideas. Start with a compelling first tweet that makes people want to read more. Number your tweets and end with a summary or call-to-action. Pin your best threads to your profile to showcase your thinking.

Use Twitter to engage with conversations already happening in your space. Reply to tweets from influencers in your field with thoughtful additions, not shameless self-promotion. Retweet with commentary that adds value. Quote tweet to share your perspective on trending topics.

★ Pro Tip: Write 5-10 valuable tweets for every 1 promotional tweet. Your promotional content performs better when it's surrounded by content that serves your audience instead of yourself.

Instagram requires visual storytelling, but that doesn't mean you can't market business books effectively. Share photos of your writing process, quote graphics from your book, behind-the-scenes glimpses of your research, and personal moments that connect with your audience.

Instagram Stories disappear after 24 hours, making them perfect for casual content that doesn't need to live on your profile forever. Use Stories for book updates, quick tips, polls about your writing decisions, and informal Q&A sessions with your audience.

Instagram's algorithm favors accounts that keep people on the platform longer. Create carousel posts that require swiping through multiple images. Write captions that encourage comments. Use relevant hashtags to help new people discover your content.

Facebook rewards posts that generate meaningful conversations among friends and family. Share personal stories connected to your book's topic. Ask questions that your audience wants to discuss with their networks. Create posts that people want to tag their friends in.

Facebook Groups offer opportunities to share your expertise without feeling promotional. Join groups where your target readers spend time. Answer questions, provide helpful resources, and build relationships before mentioning your book.

Content Types That Drive Book Sales

Educational carousel posts work across all visual platforms. Break down complex concepts into 5-10 slide presentations that teach something valuable. Include a slide at the end mentioning your book for people who want deeper information.

Behind-the-scenes content humanizes your expertise and builds anticipation for your book. Share photos of your research process, quotes from interviews you conducted, screenshots of positive reader feedback, or videos of you working on revisions.

Controversial opinion posts generate engagement but require careful handling. Share defensible but unpopular opinions about your industry. Explain your reasoning and invite discussion. Avoid politics unless your book addresses political topics.

Story posts that connect personal experiences to professional insights perform well across all platforms. Share failures that taught you important lessons. Describe moments when you realized something important about your field. Connect your personal journey to the transformation your book promises readers.

Question posts that tap into your audience's experiences and challenges create engagement while providing market research for your content. Ask about their biggest frustrations, their success strategies, or their opinions about industry trends.

> ▲ Caution: Don't post questions just to generate engagement. Ask questions you genuinely want answers to, and respond thoughtfully to the replies you receive.

Tutorial posts that teach skills related to your book topic provide immediate value while demonstrating your expertise. Keep tutorials simple enough to execute in a social media post but valuable enough that people save and share them.

Quote graphics from your book or related to your topic can work well when designed professionally and used sparingly. Include your name and book title in the image. Choose quotes that provide insight or inspiration, not just generic motivation.

Video content often outperforms static posts but requires more time and technical skill. Start with simple videos where you talk directly to the camera about topics related to your book. Save elaborate production for when you understand what resonates with your audience.

Hashtag Strategy That Doesn't Suck

Research hashtags like you research keywords for blog posts. Use tools like Hashtagify, RiteTag, or platform analytics to find hashtags your target audience uses. Avoid hashtags that are either too broad (everyone uses them) or too narrow (nobody searches for them).

Mix hashtag popularity levels in your posts. Include 2-3 popular hashtags that reach broad audiences, 5-7 medium-popularity hashtags that target your niche, and 1-2 unique hashtags that you create for your brand or book.

Create a branded hashtag for your book but don't expect it to trend organically. Use it consistently in your posts and encourage others to use it when sharing related content. Branded hashtags help you track conversations about your book across platforms.

Industry hashtags connect you with others in your field. Use hashtags that influencers, potential collaborators, and industry publications monitor. This expands your network beyond just potential book buyers.

Location hashtags can be valuable if your book has local relevance or if you're planning in-person events. Include your city, region, or venues where you're speaking.

Avoid hashtag stuffing that makes your posts look spammy. Instagram allows up to 30 hashtags, but 10-15 relevant hashtags often perform better than maxing out the limit. LinkedIn posts look professional with 3-5 hashtags maximum.

> ■ Danger Zone: Don't use trending hashtags that aren't related to your content just to get visibility. This damages your credibility and can get your content flagged as spam.

Platform hashtag strategies differ significantly. Instagram hashtags can be placed in comments to keep captions clean. Twitter hashtags should be integrated naturally into your text. LinkedIn hashtags work best when they're directly relevant to your industry.

Track hashtag performance and adjust your strategy based on what works. Some hashtags that seem relevant might not connect with your target audience. Others that seem too narrow might be exactly what your ideal readers search for.

Content Calendar and Scheduling Systems

Plan your social media content in monthly themes that align with your book marketing goals. Month one might focus on establishing expertise, month two on building anticipation, month three on launch preparation, and month four on launch execution.

Weekly content rhythms help you maintain consistency without constant decision-making. Monday motivation posts, Wednesday wisdom sharing, Friday behind-the-scenes content. Adjust based on when your audience is most active on each platform.

Daily posting isn't necessary on every platform, but consistency matters more than frequency. Better to post three times per week reliably than seven times sporadically. Choose a schedule you can maintain long-term.

Batch content creation saves time and mental energy. Spend one day per week creating all your social media content for the following week. Write captions, design graphics, and schedule posts so you're not scrambling daily.

Cross-platform adaptation lets you get more value from each piece of content you create. A blog post becomes a LinkedIn article, Instagram carousel, Twitter thread, and Facebook discussion starter. Adapt the format and language for each platform while maintaining the core message.

> ★ Pro Tip: Create content in 90-day cycles tied to your book marketing phases. This gives you enough variety to avoid repetition while maintaining focus on your current priorities.

Social media scheduling tools like Buffer, Hootsuite, or Later can automate posting and help you maintain consistency. But don't automate everything. Reserve time for real-time engagement and responses to comments and messages.

Leave room in your calendar for timely content that responds to industry news, trending topics, or opportunities that arise. A completely rigid content calendar prevents you from capitalizing on unexpected opportunities.

Monitor your analytics to understand when your audience is most active and engaged. Post timing can affect reach and engagement, but optimal times vary by platform and audience.

Engagement Strategies That Build Real Relationships

Respond to comments on your posts within a few hours when possible. Thank people for insights, answer questions thoroughly, and continue conversations that add value. Your responsiveness determines whether casual followers become engaged community members.

Engage with other people's content before expecting them to engage with yours. Like, comment, and share posts from others in your field. Build relationships through genuine interaction, not just broadcast marketing.

Ask follow-up questions in your responses to comments. This extends conversations and shows that you're genuinely interested in your audience's perspectives. Longer comment threads signal to algorithms that your content generates meaningful engagement.

Share and comment on posts from your audience members, especially when they're discussing topics related to your book. This builds goodwill and often leads to reciprocal sharing of your content.

Create content that encourages user-generated content. Ask people to share their experiences, tag friends who need to hear your message, or use your branded hashtag when posting related content.

Join conversations in comments on posts from influencers in your field. Thoughtful comments on popular posts can expose you to new audiences who are already interested in your topic.

Direct message people who leave insightful comments or who might be good connections for your broader goals. Social media can be a starting point for relationships that extend beyond any single platform.

Host live sessions where you answer questions, share insights, or discuss topics related to your book. Live content often receives algorithmic boosts and creates opportunities for real-time interaction with your audience.

Measuring What Matters for Book Marketing

Vanity metrics like followers and likes feel good but don't translate to book sales. Focus on metrics that indicate genuine interest and engagement: comments, saves, shares, and click-throughs to your website or book listings.

Track traffic from social media to your book sales pages using UTM parameters or platform analytics. This shows you which platforms and post types drive potential book buyers to take action.

Monitor mentions of your book title, author name, and branded hashtags across platforms. Tools like Mention, Hootsuite, or simple Google Alerts help you track conversations you might otherwise miss.

Engagement rate matters more than total engagement numbers. A post with 50 meaningful comments from your target audience is more valuable than a post with 500 likes from random accounts.

Save rates on Instagram and Pinterest indicate that people want to reference your content later. High save rates suggest your content provides lasting value, which correlates with interest in your book.

Comment quality reveals whether you're attracting your target audience. Comments that ask thoughtful questions, share relevant experiences, or request additional information suggest you're reaching people who might buy your book.

Click-through rates on links in your posts show whether your social media content drives traffic to your book sales pages, email signup forms, or blog posts that support your book marketing.

> ★ Pro Tip: Create a simple spreadsheet to track monthly metrics across platforms. Look for trends and patterns instead of focusing on daily fluctuations.

Email signups generated through social media often become your most engaged subscribers and likely book buyers. Track how many people join your email list through social media channels versus other sources.

Long-term relationship building shows up in repeat engagement from the same accounts. People who consistently like, comment, and share your content are building relationships that extend beyond social media.

Social media marketing for books requires patience and consistency. The platforms and tactics change constantly, but the fundamentals remain the same: provide value, build relationships, and remember that social media is just one part of a larger marketing strategy that should drive people to your book and other offerings.

Your blog established your expertise and your book demonstrates your authority. Social media helps you find and nurture the people who need what you're offering. Use it strategically, measure what matters, and remember that every meaningful connection starts with a conversation.

"Writing a book with a co-author is like getting married for a business deal. It can be beautiful and profitable, or it can end with lawyers dividing up your intellectual property and neither of you speaking to each other." - Author who learned this lesson twice

---

Writing a book doesn't have to be a solo endeavor. Some of the most successful blog-to-book conversions happen when bloggers team up with co-authors, contributors, or strategic partners who bring complementary skills, audiences, or expertise to the project.

But collaboration can also turn into a nightmare of conflicting visions, unclear responsibilities, and legal disputes that make you wish you'd tackled the project alone. The difference between productive collaboration and expensive disaster usually comes down to planning, communication, and having clear agreements about who does what.

This chapter covers the practical realities of working with others on your book project: finding the right partners, structuring agreements that protect everyone involved, managing the creative process when multiple people have opinions, and handling the business side of shared projects.

Types of Book Collaborations

Co-authoring means sharing primary writing responsibilities with one or more other people. You're all listed as authors on the cover and share equally in the creative process and business outcomes. This works best when collaborators have complementary expertise or audiences that together create something neither could produce alone.

The classic co-authoring scenario pairs domain expertise with writing ability. Maybe you're a technical expert who struggles with clear explanations, and your co-author is a professional writer who understands your field. Maybe you're both experts in different aspects of the same broad topic and want to create a comprehensive guide.

Co-authoring can also combine different audience bases. If you blog about marketing for restaurants and your potential co-author blogs about restaurant operations, a joint book about running successful restaurants might reach both audiences and provide more complete value than either of you could create individually.

Contributing authors provide chapters, case studies, or sections to your book while you maintain primary authorship and editorial control. This is less collaborative than co-authoring but more structured than just including quotes or examples from other experts.

Contributor arrangements work well for books that benefit from multiple perspectives or specialized knowledge. A book about entrepreneurship might include contributed chapters from successful entrepreneurs in different industries. A guide to content marketing might feature case studies written by practitioners using different approaches.

Ghost collaborators help with research, writing, or editing but aren't credited as authors. This includes ghostwriters who help you write the book, researchers who gather information and examples, and editors who substantially restructure or rewrite your content.

Ghost collaboration makes sense when you want to maintain your personal brand as the sole author but need help with certain aspects of the writing process. Just make sure your agreements clearly define what level of contribution requires authorship credit versus payment for services.

Strategic partnerships involve working with people or organizations that don't contribute directly to writing but provide other valuable resources. This might include research institutions that provide data, companies that offer case studies, or influencers who provide endorsements and marketing support.

Finding the Right Collaborators

Start with your existing network before reaching out to strangers. Fellow bloggers in your field, people you've met at conferences, colleagues from your professional life, or experts you've interviewed for your blog all represent potential collaboration opportunities.

The best collaborators bring complementary strengths instead of duplicate skills. If you're strong on strategy but weak on tactics, find someone who excels at practical implementation. If you understand the theory but lack real-world experience, partner with someone who has extensive field experience.

Evaluate potential collaborators based on their work quality, not just their credentials or follower counts. Read their blog posts, watch their presentations, or review their previous publications. You'll be working closely with this person for months, so make sure you respect their thinking and communication style.

Consider audience compatibility when evaluating potential partners. Do their blog readers overlap with yours in helpful ways, or would you be targeting completely different markets? Either can work, but it affects your marketing strategy and the book's positioning.

> ★ Pro Tip: Before proposing a collaboration, engage meaningfully with potential partners' content. Comment on their blog posts, share their work, and build a relationship before suggesting working together.

Professional reliability matters more than genius-level insights. You need someone who meets deadlines, communicates clearly, and handles feedback professionally. A brilliant collaborator who disappears for weeks at a time will derail your project.

Look for people whose communication style complements yours. If you're a big-picture thinker, partner with someone who excels at details. If you prefer structured approaches, find someone comfortable with iterative development. Different styles can strengthen the final product if managed well.

Avoid collaborating with people who want to use your project primarily to promote their own separate agenda. Good collaborators are committed to making the joint project successful, not just extracting value for their individual purposes.

Structuring Collaboration Agreements

Written agreements prevent most collaboration disasters. Even when working with friends or close colleagues, document your understanding about responsibilities, decision-making, credit, and financial arrangements before you start writing.

Define each person's responsibilities clearly. Who writes which chapters? Who handles research? Who manages the publishing process? Who leads marketing efforts? Vague agreements about "working together" cause conflicts when deadline pressure mounts.

Establish decision-making authority for different aspects of the project. Who has final say on the table of contents? Who approves the cover design? What happens if collaborators disagree about major editorial decisions? You can't anticipate every possible conflict, but you can create frameworks for resolving them.

Credit arrangements should be decided early and documented clearly. Will all collaborators be listed as co-authors with equal billing? Will one person be the primary author with others listed as contributors? How will contributors be acknowledged in the book's acknowledgments and marketing materials?

Financial terms need explicit agreements about costs and revenue sharing. Who pays for editing, cover design, and marketing expenses? How are book royalties divided? What happens if one collaborator wants to invest more money in marketing than others are comfortable with?

Intellectual property ownership requires clear definition, especially for books based on existing blog content. If you're both contributing posts from your respective blogs, who owns what after the book is published? Can you each continue using your contributed content in other projects?

Exit clauses should address what happens if someone wants to leave the project or if the collaboration isn't working. Can remaining collaborators continue the project? How are completed work and expenses handled if the project is abandoned?

Timeline agreements keep everyone accountable and prevent projects from dragging on indefinitely. Set deadlines for major milestones: outline completion, first draft, revisions, and final manuscript. Include consequences for missing deadlines without valid reasons.

Managing the Creative Process

Collaborative writing requires more structure than solo projects. You can't just start writing and see where inspiration takes you when multiple people need to coordinate their efforts. Invest time upfront in planning the process and communication methods.

Create a detailed outline before anyone starts writing. This isn't just chapter titles, but bullet points covering what each section will address, what examples you'll use, and how different chapters connect to each other. The outline becomes your roadmap when writers work on different sections simultaneously.

Establish style guidelines that ensure consistency across different writers' contributions. This includes voice and tone decisions, formatting preferences, how you'll handle citations and references, and any industry terminology you want to use consistently.

Use collaborative writing tools that allow real-time editing and commenting. Google Docs works for most projects, but specialized tools like Notion, Scrivener, or even GitHub can provide better organization for complex projects with multiple contributors.

Regular check-ins prevent small problems from becoming major conflicts. Schedule weekly or bi-weekly calls to review progress, discuss challenges, and make decisions about changes to the original plan. Don't wait until someone is struggling to address issues.

Version control becomes crucial when multiple people are editing the same document. Establish clear protocols about who can edit what when, how you'll track changes, and how you'll merge different versions if people work on the same sections independently.

Feedback processes need explicit structure to prevent hurt feelings and endless revision cycles. Decide whether you'll provide comments on each other's work as you go or wait until sections are complete. Agree on how to handle suggestions that one writer loves and another hates.

Editorial authority should be clearly defined to prevent conflicts about style, content, and structure decisions. Either designate one person as the final editor or create a process for resolving disagreements when they arise.

> ★ Pro Tip: Create shared documents that track decisions, style choices, and project status. This prevents repetitive discussions and ensures everyone has access to the same information.

Managing Different Writing Styles

Good collaboration often combines different writing strengths, but those differences can create inconsistency if not managed carefully. The goal isn't to make everyone write identically, but to create a cohesive final product that feels like one book, not a collection of separate essays.

Voice unification can happen during editing instead of initial writing. Let each contributor write in their natural style for first drafts, then have one person (preferably the strongest editor) revise everything for consistency in the final draft.

Content organization affects voice more than individual writing style. If your book has a clear logical progression and each section serves a purpose, readers will accept some variation in how different sections are written.

Strengths-based allocation means assigning writing tasks based on what each person does best instead of dividing work equally. If one collaborator excels at explaining complex concepts while another is better at storytelling, structure the book to use these different strengths.

Examples and case studies can maintain individual voices while serving the book's overall purpose. Let each contributor develop examples from their own experience, but ensure these examples support the same key points and conclusions.

Editing passes by different people can catch different types of problems. Have the detail-oriented person check for consistency and accuracy. Have the big-picture thinker review for flow and logic. Have the strong writer polish the language and pacing.

Reader testing with people outside your collaboration can identify inconsistencies that you've become blind to. Fresh readers will notice jarring transitions, contradictory advice, or confusing organization that seems fine to people deeply involved in the project.

Business and Legal Considerations

Publishing agreements become more complex when multiple authors are involved. Each collaborator needs to sign agreements with publishing platforms, and you need clarity about who has authority to make changes to book details, pricing, and distribution.

Copyright ownership of collaborative works can be complicated, especially when collaborators contribute existing material from their blogs. Consult with attorneys familiar with publishing law if your collaboration involves substantial existing intellectual property or significant financial potential.

Tax implications of collaboration income depend on how you structure the partnership and divide revenue. Each collaborator is typically responsible for their own taxes on book income, but complex arrangements might require formal business partnerships or other structures.

Revenue tracking and distribution require systems for monitoring book sales across platforms and ensuring everyone receives their agreed-upon share. Simple arrangements can be handled manually, but successful books might require more sophisticated financial management.

Marketing responsibilities need clear definition because book promotion affects everyone's reputation and financial success. Who manages social media? Who handles media interviews? Who pays for advertising campaigns?

> ■ Danger Zone: Don't assume that collaboration means everyone has to participate equally in all aspects of marketing. Some people are comfortable with public speaking while others prefer written promotion. Play to strengths instead of forcing equal participation.

Ongoing obligations extend beyond the book's publication. Will collaborators jointly handle reader questions and support? Who manages updates and revised editions? What happens if one person wants to write a sequel and others don't?

Dispute resolution mechanisms should be established before conflicts arise. Mediation clauses, arbitration agreements, or simple processes for handling disagreements can prevent small problems from destroying relationships and projects.

Success metrics should be defined jointly so everyone is working toward the same goals. Are you primarily focused on book sales, building platform, generating speaking opportunities, or establishing credibility? Different priorities can create conflicts if not addressed explicitly.

Making Collaboration Work Long-Term

Successful collaborations often lead to additional projects, but only if the first experience is positive for everyone involved. Building good working relationships requires attention to both the business and personal aspects of partnership.

Communication preferences vary between people. Some prefer detailed emails while others want quick phone calls. Some need advance notice of deadlines while others work better under pressure. Learn your collaborators' preferences and adapt your communication style accordingly.

Appreciation and recognition help maintain positive relationships throughout stressful project timelines. Acknowledge your collaborators' contributions publicly, thank them for good work privately, and give credit generously when discussing the project with others.

Flexibility about changing circumstances keeps projects moving when life interferes with original plans. Health issues, family emergencies, or professional obligations can affect anyone's ability to meet original commitments. Build buffer time into your schedule and be prepared to adjust roles if necessary.

Learning from each project makes future collaborations more successful. After completing your book, conduct a retrospective discussion about what worked well, what could be improved, and what you'd do differently next time.

Network expansion happens naturally through collaboration but can be amplified through intentional relationship building. Introduce your collaborators to your professional network and ask them to do the same. Good collaborations open doors that none of you could access individually.

Future opportunities often arise from successful collaborations. Your book project might lead to speaking opportunities, consulting engagements, or additional book deals that benefit all collaborators. Maintain relationships even after your immediate project is complete.

Collaboration amplifies both the potential benefits and risks of book publishing. When it works well, you create better books, reach larger audiences, and build valuable professional relationships. When it goes wrong, you waste time, damage relationships, and sometimes create legal complications.

The key to successful collaboration is treating it like any other business partnership: clear agreements, regular communication, mutual respect, and shared commitment to the project's success. Your blog established your individual expertise, but collaboration can help you create something larger and more valuable than any of you could achieve alone.

Choose collaborators wisely, structure agreements carefully, and remember that the best partnerships enhance everyone's individual strengths while creating collective value that exceeds the sum of its parts.

"The biggest mistake most authors make is thinking their book is a product. Your book isn't a product, it's a very expensive business card that happens to generate royalties." - Publishing strategist explaining why most authors stay broke

---

Most authors think book sales are the endgame. You write the book, people buy it, you collect royalties. That's like thinking a business card is meant to generate revenue instead of starting conversations that lead to revenue.

Your book is a business card, not a business. A good, expensive business card that demonstrates your expertise and opens doors that would otherwise remain closed. Smart authors understand this and build monetization strategies that treat book sales as the beginning of the revenue story, not the end.

This chapter covers advanced monetization strategies that extend far beyond Amazon royalties: licensing your content, selling foreign rights, developing bulk sales channels, creating high-value derivative products, and building long-term revenue streams that compound over years.

Beyond Basic Book Sales

Direct sales through your own channels often generate higher profit margins than platform sales, but they require more marketing effort and infrastructure investment. Selling books through your website, at speaking events, or through professional networks can double your per-unit profit while building direct relationships with buyers.

Your website sales don't compete with Amazon sales, they complement them. People who are already familiar with your work and actively seek you out are willing to buy directly. Use platform sales to reach new audiences and direct sales to serve your existing community.

Speaking engagements provide natural opportunities for book sales, often at premium prices. Attendees at conferences and workshops are predisposed to buy from speakers they've just heard. A $15 book becomes a $25 book when sold at the back of the room after a compelling presentation.

Corporate sales to organizations that want to distribute your book to employees, customers, or partners can generate substantial revenue from single transactions. A company buying 500 copies for their team pays the same wholesale price per book but creates one large transaction instead of 500 individual sales.

Educational markets, including universities, training companies, and professional organizations, often purchase books in quantities and at price points that individual consumers won't. A book that retails for $19.99 to people might sell for $35 to institutions that value the content for training purposes.

Subscription box services, book clubs, and other curated distribution channels can expose your book to audiences you'd never reach through traditional marketing. These channels typically take significant cuts of the revenue, but they handle all marketing and distribution logistics.

★ Pro Tip: Create special editions or bonus materials exclusively for direct sales channels. This gives people reasons to buy from you instead of Amazon while providing higher value that justifies premium pricing.

Licensing and Syndication Opportunities

Content licensing allows other organizations to use your book's material in their own products, training programs, or publications. This generates revenue without requiring additional work from you while extending your book's reach into markets you couldn't access directly.

Corporate training companies often license book content to incorporate into their curriculum development. Your chapter about leadership communication might become part of a management training program sold to Fortune 500 companies. Your marketing frameworks might be licensed by consulting firms for client workshops.

Educational publishers sometimes license content from successful business books for inclusion in textbooks or course materials. Academic markets pay higher prices than consumer markets and provide steady revenue streams for content that remains relevant across multiple school years.

Media companies, including magazines, websites, and podcast networks, may license excerpts or adapted versions of your content for their audiences. This provides exposure that drives book sales while generating licensing fees.

Software companies developing training platforms or educational apps sometimes license book content to provide educational materials within their products. Your book about productivity might become the foundation for a productivity app's educational content.

International licensing allows publishers in other countries to translate and distribute your book in their markets. While you could handle international distribution yourself, working with established local publishers often generates more revenue with less effort.

Syndication through content networks can distribute your book's key concepts through multiple channels simultaneously. Business publications, training companies, and online learning platforms all need quality content and are willing to pay for proven materials.

> ▲ Caution: Licensing agreements should clearly define usage rights, territory restrictions, and revenue sharing arrangements. Consider working with agents or attorneys experienced in publishing contracts for complex licensing deals.

Foreign Rights and International Markets

Translation rights represent significant revenue opportunities for books that address universal business or personal development topics. Markets like Germany, Japan, and Brazil have substantial audiences for English-language business content translated into local languages.

Foreign publishers handle translation, local marketing, and distribution in exchange for paying you advances and royalties. This allows you to enter international markets without learning foreign languages or understanding local business customs.

The foreign rights market operates differently from domestic publishing. Rights are often sold at international book fairs, through specialized agents, or via direct relationships with foreign publishers. Building these relationships takes time but can generate substantial long-term revenue.

Some topics translate better than others across cultures. Technical skills, productivity systems, and business frameworks often work globally with minor adaptations. Content that relies heavily on cultural references, local regulations, or market conditions requires more significant adaptation.

Advance payments for foreign rights can range from a few thousand dollars for smaller markets to six figures for major territories and popular topics. These advances are paid upon signing, providing immediate revenue while the translation and publication process unfolds over months or years.

Territory editions allow you to adapt content for different markets while maintaining control over the adaptation process. This requires more work than simple translation but can result in better-performing books and higher revenue shares.

Digital-first foreign distribution through international ebook platforms can test market demand before investing in translation and print distribution. Strong digital sales in a territory indicate potential for full foreign rights deals.

> ■ Danger Zone: Don't grant exclusive worldwide rights to any single publisher unless they're offering substantial advances and have proven ability to exploit those rights globally. Maintain flexibility to work with different publishers in different territories.

Bulk Sales and Institutional Markets

Corporate bulk sales often generate higher per-unit revenue than individual consumer sales while requiring less marketing effort per transaction. Companies buying books for employee development, customer gifts, or conference giveaways care more about content quality than price optimization.

Minimum order quantities for bulk sales typically start at 50-100 copies, but meaningful discounts usually begin at 500+ copies. The economics work because you're trading volume for margin, but the absolute profit per transaction increases substantially.

Government agencies, including military branches, federal departments, and local government organizations, purchase books for training and development programs. These markets move slowly but pay premium prices and offer steady demand for quality content.

Professional associations buy books for member benefits, conference materials, and continuing education programs. Association sales often lead to speaking opportunities and additional marketing exposure within industries.

Training companies and consultants purchase books to use as course materials or client resources. They're willing to pay higher prices because they're incorporating your content into higher-value services they sell to their clients.

Non-profit organizations sometimes purchase books for fundraising purposes, donor gifts, or program materials. While non-profits are price-sensitive, they often value content that aligns with their mission and are willing to support authors who share their values.

Bulk sales require different marketing approaches than individual consumer sales. Direct outreach to decision-makers, relationship building through industry networks, and demonstrating ROI for organizational goals matter more than typical book marketing tactics.

★ Pro Tip: Create supplementary materials for bulk purchasers: discussion guides, implementation worksheets, or presentation slides that add value for organizations using your book in group settings.

Creating High-Value Derivative Products

Online courses based on your book's content can generate substantially more revenue than book sales while serving customers who prefer interactive learning experiences. A $19.99 book can become a $499 course that provides implementation support and community interaction.

Course development requires additional work, but much of the content already exists in your book. The course structure, learning objectives, and core teaching points are already developed. You're adding video content, exercises, and student interaction instead of creating entirely new material.

Workshops and training programs allow you to deliver your book's content in person or virtually for premium pricing. A one-day workshop based on your book might generate more revenue than months of book sales while building relationships with participants who become long-term customers.

Certification programs based on your book's methodology can create ongoing revenue streams while building communities of practitioners who promote your work. Participants pay for training, testing, and ongoing certification maintenance.

Software tools that implement your book's systems or frameworks can generate subscription revenue while making your concepts more practical for readers. A book about project management might spawn a project management app. A productivity book might become a productivity software platform.

Membership communities focused on implementing your book's concepts provide ongoing revenue through monthly or annual subscriptions. Members get access to updated content, expert discussions, and peer support for applying your methodology.

Coaching and consulting services positioned as extensions of your book's expertise command premium pricing because your book has already demonstrated your knowledge and approach. Clients who've read your book are pre-qualified and understand your methods.

Speaking opportunities often pay $5,000 to $50,000 per engagement for authors of successful business books. Your book serves as an extended audition tape that demonstrates your expertise and presentation ability to event organizers.

Long-Term Revenue Strategies

Evergreen content in rapidly changing fields requires ongoing updates and revisions to maintain relevance and sales momentum. Plan for revised editions that incorporate new developments, updated examples, and expanded content based on reader feedback.

Series development allows you to build on your initial book's success with related titles that serve the same audience. Each subsequent book benefits from the credibility and audience established by previous titles while addressing different aspects of your expertise.

Platform licensing enables other content creators to use your frameworks, terminology, or methodologies in their own work in exchange for fees or revenue sharing. This turns your intellectual property into a scalable business asset.

Media rights for your book's content might be valuable if your story or expertise attracts attention from documentary makers, podcast producers, or other media companies. While most books don't generate significant media rights revenue, successful books sometimes attract unexpected opportunities.

Legacy revenue streams can continue generating income for years or decades after publication. Books that become standard references in their fields, required reading for certification programs, or foundational texts for training curricula provide steady long-term income.

Acquisition opportunities sometimes arise when larger companies or publishers want to acquire successful book-based businesses. Your book and its derivative products might become acquisition targets if they demonstrate sustainable competitive advantages.

Estate planning for intellectual property ensures that your book's revenue potential continues benefiting your heirs. Copyright protection lasts for decades beyond your lifetime, and successful books can provide ongoing income for your estate.

Building Sustainable Revenue Models

Diversified revenue streams reduce dependence on any single source while maximizing the value of your intellectual property investment. Your book becomes the foundation for multiple income sources instead of just one product.

Customer lifetime value optimization focuses on converting book buyers into higher-value customers for your other products and services. A $20 book buyer might become a $2,000 course purchaser or a $20,000 consulting client.

Recurring revenue models provide more predictable income than one-time book sales. Membership sites, subscription services, and ongoing training programs create monthly or annual revenue that compounds naturally.

Scalable systems allow you to generate increasing revenue without proportionally increasing your time investment. Once created, online courses, licensing agreements, and certification programs can serve unlimited customers with minimal additional effort.

Brand building through your book establishes you as the recognized authority in your niche, which increases demand for all your products and services while allowing you to charge premium prices.

Strategic partnerships with complementary businesses can extend your book's reach while creating new revenue opportunities. Training companies, software providers, and consulting firms might all represent partnership opportunities.

Your book represents an investment in long-term business development, not just immediate revenue generation. The most successful authors treat their books as foundations for larger business strategies that create value across multiple channels and time horizons.

Think beyond the book sale to the business environment your book enables. The real money often comes from what your book makes possible, not from what your book generates directly. Build accordingly, and your blog-to-book conversion becomes the foundation for sustainable, scalable revenue that extends far beyond anything you imagined when you first considered organizing your blog posts into chapters.

The authors who treat their books as products focus on sales optimization and marketing efficiency. The authors who treat their books as platforms focus on relationship building and business development. Both approaches can work, but only one builds lasting competitive advantages that compound naturally.

Your expertise deserves more than book royalties. Use these advanced monetization strategies to create the business outcomes that justify the investment you've made in converting your blog content into book-length authority.

"The most expensive education is experience, but the most valuable education is someone else's experience." -- Mark Twain, who probably would have had a terrible blog-to-book conversion rate in today's market

---

Every blogger who considers writing a book should study both the victories and the disasters that came before them. Success stories inspire us and show what's possible. Failure stories teach us what to avoid and often provide more practical wisdom than any amount of theoretical advice.

This chapter examines real blog-to-book conversions: the spectacular successes, the expensive failures, and the lessons learned from both. These aren't theoretical examples or hypothetical scenarios. These are real people who invested real time and money in converting their blog content into books, with outcomes that range from life-changing success to financial catastrophe.

The Success Stories

Case Study 1: From Anonymous Waiter to Published Author

The Blog: Waiter Rant started as exactly what it sounds like: a disgruntled restaurant server venting about customers, management, and the service industry. The anonymous blogger shared stories from his shifts at an upscale restaurant, mixing humor with insider insights about what really happens behind kitchen doors.

What Made It Work: The blog succeeded because it provided an authentic insider's perspective that readers couldn't get anywhere else. The author didn't try to be polite or politically correct. He shared the unfiltered truth about restaurant culture, difficult customers, and the realities of service work. His writing voice was conversational, funny, and relatable to anyone who had ever worked in customer service.

The blog built a devoted following of restaurant workers who recognized their own experiences in his stories, and curious outsiders who enjoyed the behind-the-scenes glimpse into a world they thought they understood but really didn't. Comments sections became communities where service industry workers shared their own horror stories and supported each other.

> ★ Pro Tip: Authenticity beats polish when you're sharing insider perspectives. Readers can tell when you're sanitizing your experience for broader appeal.

The Book Conversion: When the blog attracted traditional publisher attention, the author faced a unique challenge: how do you turn episodic rants into a cohesive book? The solution was organizing the content around the restaurant hierarchy and the progression of a typical shift, using individual blog stories as examples within larger themes.

The book wasn't just a collection of blog posts. It included new material that provided context for outsiders, explained industry jargon, and offered a more complete picture of restaurant culture. The author maintained his authentic voice while creating something that worked for readers who had never seen the blog.

Why It Succeeded:

- Unique perspective from inside a world most people only see as customers
- Authentic voice that refused to sanitize experience for broader appeal
- Community building that created a space where service workers felt understood
- Perfect timing during a period when food culture was becoming mainstream entertainment

- Professional execution that maintained authenticity while improving readability

Results: The book became a bestseller, led to media appearances, and established the author as a commentator on service industry issues. More importantly, it validated the experiences of countless service workers who felt invisible in discussions about restaurant culture.

Case Study 2: The Happiness Project (Testing Ideas Through Blogging)

The Blog: Gretchen Rubin didn't exactly blog her book, but she used her blog as a laboratory for the ideas that would eventually become "The Happiness Project." She wrote about her experiments with different approaches to increasing happiness, shared research findings, and engaged with readers about their own happiness challenges.

What Made It Work: Rubin approached happiness like a research project instead of a feel-good inspiration fest. She tested concrete strategies, measured results, and reported honestly about what worked and what didn't. Her blog posts weren't polished conclusions but works in progress, letting readers follow along with her thinking.

The blog served as both content development and market research. Reader comments revealed which concepts resonated, which explanations needed clarification, and which approaches people were most eager to try themselves. By the time she wrote the book, she had already tested her ideas with thousands of people.

The Book Conversion: The book organized her scattered experiments into a systematic year-long project with clear monthly themes and practical strategies. She didn't just copy blog posts; she synthesized her learning into a replicable framework that readers could adapt to their own lives.

The blog content provided raw material, but the book provided structure, progression, and completion that individual posts couldn't offer. Readers who had followed the blog still found value in seeing the complete picture and getting the refined strategies.

> ▲ Caution: Don't assume blog readers will automatically buy your book. Even loyal followers need compelling reasons to pay for content they've been getting free.

Why It Succeeded:

- Evidence-based approach that used research and personal experimentation instead of vague platitudes
- Reader engagement that involved audience in developing and testing ideas
- Clear methodology that created a systematic approach readers could follow
- Universal appeal that addressed fundamental human desire for happiness
- Authentic reporting that shared failures and limitations along with successes

Results: The book became a multi-million-copy bestseller, spawned sequels, and established Rubin as a happiness expert. The blog continued to drive book sales while the book brought new readers to the blog, creating a virtuous cycle that sustained both platforms.

Case Study 3: How to Blog a Book (Teaching What You're Learning)

The Blog: Nina Amir started blogging about the process of writing a book through blog posts while she was doing it. Her blog documented her experiments with different approaches, shared tools and techniques she discovered, and built a community of writers interested in the same process.

What Made It Work: Amir didn't wait until she was an expert to start teaching. She shared her learning in real-time, which made her content more relatable and practical than traditional writing advice from established authors. Her approach was systematic and practical: she wasn't just documenting her journey, she was creating a methodology others could follow.

The blog attracted writers who were struggling with the same challenges, creating a community of practice around blog-to-book conversion. Readers contributed their own experiments and results, which provided additional content and validation for the approach.

The Book Conversion: The book organized her blog content into a step-by-step guide that newcomers could follow without needing to read years of blog posts. She added frameworks, worksheets, and resources that provided more structure than the blog format allowed.

The book also included case studies from other bloggers who had successfully converted their content, which added credibility and showed different paths to the same goal. This wasn't just one person's experience anymore, it was a proven methodology with multiple examples.

Why It Succeeded:

- Practical focus that provided practical strategies instead of inspirational platitudes
- Community building that created space for writers to share experiences and support each other
- Systematic approach that developed replicable frameworks instead of one-off tactics
- Proof of concept that demonstrated the method by using it successfully herself
- Ongoing evolution that continued improving the methodology based on reader feedback

Results: The book became the definitive guide to blog-to-book conversion, leading to speaking opportunities, coaching services, and a thriving business built around helping writers succeed. The blog continued to generate new content that supported book sales while establishing Amir as the leading authority on the topic.

The Failure Stories

Case Study 1: The $1,900 Launch That Earned $150

The Author: Ron Vitale had been blogging successfully about writing and had published several books in different series. His blog had built credibility in the writing community, and his previous books had found modest success with their target audiences.

The Book: "Ahab's Daughter" was a fantasy adventure novel featuring Captain Ahab's daughter searching for her lost brother. Despite having a loyal blog following and experience with book launches, this project became an expensive lesson in misunderstanding audience and market dynamics.

What Went Wrong: Vitale made several critical errors that turned a promising project into a financial disaster.

Audience Mismatch: His existing blog readers and book buyers were interested in his established fantasy and romance series, but "Ahab's Daughter" represented a significant departure in tone and style. He assumed his platform would transfer to any fantasy story, but audiences are often more specific than authors realize. A reader who loves contemporary fairy tale retellings isn't automatically interested in high-seas adventure just because they like the author.

Standalone Launch Strategy: Instead of launching a series, he published a single book and expected it to find its audience independently. As he later admitted: "It's really difficult to get new readers to jump into book 1, especially if you're trying a new genre."

> ■ Danger Zone: Never launch a standalone book in a genre that's new for you. Your existing audience may not follow, and new readers have no reason to trust you yet.

Over-Investment in Marketing: He spent heavily on professional services and advertising without validating market demand first:

- Cover design: $381
- Copy editing: $441
- Book description revision: $157
- Review services: $212
- Advertising campaigns: $682
- Total investment: $1,907.63

Poor Series Planning: His most effective strategy would have been writing books 2 and 3 before launching, then releasing them three months apart to maintain momentum. Instead, he published book 1 and hoped it would succeed on its own.

The Results: Despite professional production values and significant marketing investment, the book sold only enough to generate $151.78 in royalties. The disconnect between investment and return was devastating, especially considering the book received exclusively 5-star reviews from the few readers who found it.

What This Teaches Us:

- Platform loyalty doesn't automatically transfer across different story types or tones
- Professional production can't compensate for fundamental market misalignment
- Single book launches in new territories are extremely difficult for indie authors
- Market validation should happen before major investment, not after
- Even excellent books can fail commercially if they don't reach the right readers

Case Study 2: The Expert's Invisible Book

The Pattern: This represents multiple failed blog-to-book conversions where subject matter experts assumed their expertise automatically translated to book success.

The Typical Setup: These bloggers had impressive credentials and deep knowledge in their fields. Their blogs attracted small but engaged audiences of fellow experts. When they converted their content to books, they made critical positioning errors that doomed their projects.

What Went Wrong:

Undefined Audience: When asked who their book was for, these authors invariably answered "smart people" or "anyone interested in [complex topic]." They couldn't articulate who would buy their book or why, which made marketing impossible.

Academic Blindness: They assumed readers had the same background knowledge and interest level they did. Their books required extensive prior knowledge to understand, but they never explained why non-experts should care about their topic.

Expert Language: They wrote for peer review instead of popular consumption, using jargon and theoretical frameworks that alienated general readers without providing enough depth for true experts.

> ▲ Caution: Expertise alone doesn't create book success. Every book needs a clearly defined target reader who has specific problems your book solves.

The Results: These books typically sold fewer than 100 copies, mostly to friends, family, and professional colleagues. Despite containing valuable information, they failed to find markets because they weren't designed for any audience's real needs.

What This Teaches Us:

- Professional knowledge must be translated, not just transferred
- Books must solve problems or fulfill desires for defined audiences
- Academic voice and popular writing require completely different approaches

- Even brilliant insights are worthless if they can't be understood or applied

Case Study 3: The Premature Blog Book

The Situation: A lifestyle blogger with six months of content and moderate traffic decided to convert their posts into a book about minimalist living.

What Went Wrong:

Insufficient Content Depth: Six months of blogging hadn't provided enough material for a substantial book. The author tried to stretch thin content across 200 pages, resulting in repetitive, shallow treatment of important topics.

Incomplete Expertise: The blogger was still learning about minimalism themselves but presented themselves as an expert in the book. Readers noticed the lack of depth and experience, leading to negative reviews that questioned the author's credibility.

Poor Content Organization: Blog posts written chronologically didn't translate into logical book structure. The author copied and pasted posts without creating bridges or ensuring coherent progression from chapter to chapter.

Premature Monetization: The rush to publish was driven by desire for revenue instead of readiness of content or audience. The blogger hadn't built sufficient platform or authority to support book sales.

The Results: The book received multiple negative reviews pointing out its superficial treatment of the topic. Sales were minimal, and the poor reviews damaged the blogger's credibility for future projects.

What This Teaches Us:

- Quality and depth matter more than speed to market
- Books require more authority and expertise than individual blog posts

- Content organization for books requires different skills than blogging
- Platform and credibility must be established before monetization
- Negative reviews can have lasting impact on author reputation

Patterns in Success and Failure

The Success Formula

Successful blog-to-book conversions share several characteristics:

Audience-First Thinking: Winners start with clear understanding of who will buy the book and why. They can articulate their target reader's problems, desires, and expectations.

Content Integration: They don't just copy and paste blog content. They reorganize, expand, and create new material that serves the book's purpose while maintaining the voice and insights that made their blog valuable.

Platform Alignment: They create mutual support between their blog and book, where each platform enhances the other. Their blogs continue generating new content that drives book sales while their books bring new readers to their blogs.

Realistic Expectations: They understand that books are part of larger business strategies, not get-rich-quick schemes. They invest appropriately in production and marketing while maintaining realistic timelines and financial expectations.

The Failure Formula

Failed conversions typically involve one or more of these mistakes:

The Expertise Trap: Experts who understand their subject deeply but can't communicate with non-experts effectively.

They write for their peers instead of their potential readers, resulting in books that are too complex for general audiences but not rigorous enough for academic ones.

The Platform Assumption: Bloggers who assume their existing audience will automatically buy their book, regardless of topic, genre, or format differences. Blog readers and book buyers have different motivations and expectations.

The Production Obsession: Authors who focus intensely on professional covers, editing, and formatting while ignoring fundamental questions about audience and market fit. Professional production values can't compensate for books that solve no problems or serve no clear purpose.

The Single-Shot Strategy: Authors who treat their book as a one-time project instead of part of a larger content strategy often struggle to generate sufficient marketing momentum.

> ★ Pro Tip: Success comes from understanding that books and blogs serve different purposes for different audiences. Your blog proves you can create valuable content, but book success requires additional strategic thinking about audience, market, and business objectives.

What This Means for Your blog-to-book process

Before you start, define your target reader in painful detail. Not demographics, but psychographics. What keeps them awake at night? What do they desperately want to achieve? How does your book help them get there?

Ensure your blog content addresses clear problems or needs. If your posts are just random thoughts or observations, you don't have book material. You have diary entries.

Validate market demand before major investment. Start with small tests: survey your audience, create a detailed outline and see if it generates interest, write sample chapters and gauge response.

Plan for ongoing content creation that supports book sales. Your book launch isn't the end of your marketing, it's the beginning.

During production, reorganize content for book format instead of just compiling posts. Write new material that serves the book's purpose. Invest in professional editing and design, but only after validating market fit.

Create marketing materials that focus on reader benefits, not author credentials. Nobody cares how smart you are; they care about how your book makes their life better.

After launch, monitor results and learn from both successes and failures. Continue creating content that supports book discoverability. Build relationships with readers who could become advocates. Plan your next project based on what you've learned.

The difference between successful and failed blog-to-book conversions often comes down to understanding that good content isn't enough. You need the right content for the right audience at the right time with the right positioning.

Your blog has already proven that you can create valuable content. Converting that content into a successful book requires additional skills, but they're skills that can be learned. Study the successes, avoid the common failures, and remember that every published author started exactly where you are now.

Most importantly, remember that failure isn't final. Many successful authors failed with their first attempts but used those experiences to create better books and more effective strategies. The key is learning from both your own experiences and the experiences of others who've walked this path before you.

Success isn't guaranteed, but it's much more likely when you understand what works, what doesn't, and why.

International Publishing Considerations

The internet has no borders, but book publishing still does. Welcome to the wonderful world of international tax forms, currency conversion, and trying to explain American slang to readers in Mumbai.

Blog-to-book advice loves to focus on the U.S. market. Makes sense: it's the largest English-language book market and Amazon's headquarters. But successful blogs attract global audiences, and books can reach readers worldwide from day one. Publishing internationally brings additional complexities and opportunities that come with crossing borders.

This chapter covers the practical realities of international publishing: platform differences, tax implications, cultural considerations, and strategies for reaching readers outside your home country. Whether you're in Toronto or Bangalore, London or Sydney, the fundamentals of blog-to-book conversion stay the same. The execution details? That's where things get interesting.

Amazon Kindle Direct Publishing operates in most major markets, but the experience varies dramatically by country. Authors in the United States, United Kingdom, Canada, and Australia get the full KDP experience: print-on-demand, expanded distribution, comprehensive royalty options. Authors elsewhere? You're getting the economy package.

KDP supports authors from over 100 countries, but availability doesn't mean equality. Authors from Germany, Japan, and India can publish ebooks globally but often face limited access to print-on-demand services or expanded distribution networks. Amazon's royalty rates vary by country and delivery method. The standard 70% royalty rate for ebooks priced between $2.99 and $9.99 applies in most major markets, but delivery charges eat into profits for authors in countries with higher data costs. Print book royalties also vary based on local printing costs and distribution arrangements.

Amazon pays royalties when your account reaches certain thresholds, which vary by country and payment method. U.S. authors receive payments at $100 for direct deposit and $100 for check. Authors in other countries face higher thresholds or additional fees for international transfers.

> ★ Pro Tip: Check Amazon's current payment policies for your country before publishing. Some regions require tax information or bank verification that can delay your first payment by months.

Draft2Digital distributes to multiple retailers worldwide and often provides better international support than going direct to each retailer. They handle format conversion, distribution logistics, and payments, making them valuable for authors who want global reach without managing multiple platform relationships. Kobo, based in Canada, has strong market presence in Canada, Australia, and several European countries. Their self-publishing platform, Kobo Writing Life, offers competitive royalty rates and often provides better visibility for non-U.S. authors than Amazon does in those markets.

Google Play Books offers global distribution and competitive royalty rates, though discoverability can be challenging. They're strong in markets where Android devices dominate, covering many developing countries. Many countries have domestic ebook retailers that beat international platforms for reaching local audiences: Chapters Indigo in Canada, Waterstones in the UK, and various platforms throughout Europe and Asia.

Print-on-demand technology has revolutionized international publishing, but significant limitations remain. Amazon's print services are available in limited countries, and shipping costs for international orders can make books prohibitively expensive for readers. IngramSpark offers broader international print distribution than Amazon, with printing facilities in multiple countries. This significantly reduces shipping costs and delivery times for international readers, but setup is more complex and expensive than Amazon's system. Some successful international authors partner with local publishers or print services in their target markets. This requires more upfront investment and logistics management but provides better market access and cost-effective distribution.

Non-U.S. authors selling through American platforms face potential tax withholding on their royalties. The default withholding rate is 30%, but tax treaties between the U.S. and many countries can reduce this to 0-15% if proper forms are filed. Authors without U.S. Social Security Numbers need Individual Taxpayer Identification Numbers (ITINs) to claim treaty benefits. The ITIN application process takes several months and requires specific documentation.

Tax treaties vary significantly between countries. Authors from the UK, Canada, and Australia often qualify for reduced or eliminated withholding, while authors from countries without tax treaties face the full 30% rate. Form W-8BEN must be completed and updated regularly to claim treaty benefits. Failing to maintain current tax information results in maximum withholding rates being applied to your royalties.

> ▲ Caution: International tax law is complex and changes regularly. Consult with tax professionals familiar with your country's treaty arrangements before making assumptions about withholding rates.

Earning income from international book sales creates tax obligations in your home country, regardless of any U.S. withholding. Most countries tax worldwide income, which means your book royalties face domestic income tax even when earned through foreign platforms. Royalties earned in foreign currencies must typically be converted to your local currency for tax purposes. Exchange rate fluctuations complicate record-keeping and tax calculations, especially when you receive payments throughout the year at different rates.

Most countries allow authors to deduct legitimate business expenses against their writing income: editing, cover design, marketing, and sometimes home office expenses. Keep detailed records and receipts for all publishing-related expenses. International tax situations can be complex enough to warrant professional advice. A tax accountant familiar with author income and international treaties can often save you more money than their fees cost.

Your blog attracted international readers, but books require different cultural sensitivity than blog posts. Readers investing money in your book expect content that speaks to their experiences, not just American cultural references and assumptions. Even within English-speaking markets, language conventions vary. British readers expect different spelling, punctuation, and terminology than American readers. Canadian and Australian readers have their own preferences. Consider creating different versions of your book for different markets if cultural references are significant.

Examples and case studies that resonate with American readers may be meaningless or alienating to international audiences. A reference to "401(k) retirement planning" means nothing to British readers, while discussion of "university fees" might confuse Americans who think in terms of "college tuition." Advice about business, finance, or legal matters varies dramatically between countries. What's legal and common in one country may be illegal or impossible in another. Include appropriate disclaimers and consider whether your advice applies globally.

A $9.99 ebook price that seems reasonable to American readers might feel expensive in countries with lower average incomes or different purchasing power. Research local market pricing and consider whether uniform global pricing serves your goals. Most platforms automatically display prices in local currencies, but the conversion may not reflect local market realities. A book priced at $9.99 USD becomes approximately £8 or €9, but local market conditions might suggest different optimal price points. Discount promotions and marketing strategies that work in one market may not translate to others. Holiday seasons, shopping patterns, and promotional expectations vary significantly between countries.

Social media platform popularity varies dramatically by country. While Facebook and Twitter have global reach, platforms like WeChat, WhatsApp, TikTok, and region-specific networks may be more effective for reaching audiences in certain countries. Scheduling social media posts, email campaigns, and promotional activities requires consideration of when your target audiences are online. A promotion timed for U.S. Pacific Time may completely miss your European or Asian audiences. Marketing copy that works in one culture may fall flat or offend in another. Direct sales language common in American marketing can seem pushy or inappropriate in cultures that prefer more subtle approaches.

Building relationships with bloggers, podcasters, and media personalities in your target markets beats trying to reach international audiences through U.S.-based promotion. Book review blogs and BookTube channels exist in most countries and languages. Research and build relationships with influencers who reach your target demographics in specific countries. Literary festivals, book fairs, and author events happen worldwide. Virtual participation has made international events more accessible, providing opportunities to connect with readers and other authors globally.

> ★ Pro Tip: Join international author groups and forums specific to your genre or target markets. Local knowledge from authors already succeeding in those markets is invaluable.

Copyright protection varies between countries, though most major markets participate in international treaties that provide baseline protection. Your book is generally protected in countries that are signatories to the Berne Convention, covering most developed nations. While copyright exists automatically in most countries, registration processes and benefits vary. U.S. copyright registration provides specific legal advantages in

American courts, but may be less relevant for authors primarily operating in other countries. Enforcing copyright across international borders can be complex and expensive. Piracy and unauthorized distribution may be more challenging to address when it occurs in countries with different legal systems or enforcement priorities.

Publishing platform agreements typically specify which country's laws govern disputes and where legal action must be taken. This creates challenges for international authors who may need to pursue legal remedies in foreign courts. Platform content policies may reflect the cultural and legal standards of their home countries, which may not align with standards in your country. Content that's acceptable in your culture might violate platform policies, and vice versa.

Authors earning from multiple international platforms may receive payments in different currencies, creating complexity in financial management and planning. Currency fluctuations significantly impact your effective income. A book earning €100 per month might generate $110 one month and $95 the next, depending on exchange rates. International wire transfers often involve significant fees and delays. Some authors find it worthwhile to maintain bank accounts in major markets to reduce transfer costs and currency conversion fees. Budgeting and financial planning become more complex when income streams involve multiple currencies with fluctuating exchange rates. Consider working with financial advisors familiar with international income streams.

Success Strategies for International Authors

Market Research and Validation

Local Market Analysis: Research book markets in your target countries before assuming global demand. Genre preferences, pricing expectations, and reading habits vary significantly between markets.

Cultural Sensitivity Testing: Consider having native speakers or cultural consultants review your content before launching in new markets. Cultural misunderstandings can damage your reputation and sales prospects.

Platform Performance Monitoring: Track your book's performance across different platforms and countries. You may find that certain markets or platforms significantly outperform others, allowing you to focus your marketing efforts more effectively.

Building Sustainable International Presence

Long-term Platform Strategy: Develop relationships with multiple platforms rather than depending entirely on Amazon. Platform policies, market conditions, and competitive landscapes change constantly.

Local Partnerships: Consider partnering with local authors, publishers, or marketing professionals in key markets. Their cultural knowledge and existing networks can accelerate your market entry and reduce costly mistakes.

Continuous Learning: International markets and regulations change constantly. Stay informed about developments in your key markets through author forums, professional organizations, and industry publications.

> ■ Danger Zone: Don't assume that success in one market guarantees success in another. Each market requires specific research, cultural adaptation, and often different marketing approaches.

The opportunities for international publishing have never been better, but success requires more than just uploading your book to global platforms. Understanding the cultural, legal, and practical differences between markets allows you to make informed decisions about where to focus your efforts and how to adapt your approach for maximum effectiveness.

Your blog already demonstrated that your content can attract readers from different countries and cultures. Converting that global interest into book sales requires additional preparation and cultural sensitivity, but the potential rewards (both financial and in terms of impact) make the effort worthwhile.

Start with realistic expectations about the additional complexity involved while remaining excited about the opportunity to reach readers worldwide. Your ideas and expertise aren't limited by geography, and neither should your publishing strategy be.

Take the time to understand the markets you want to enter, adapt your content and marketing appropriately, and remember that building international success typically takes longer than domestic success but provides more sustainable and diverse income streams.

The world is full of readers who could benefit from your expertise and perspective. International publishing gives you the tools to reach them, but success depends on respecting their cultures, understanding their markets, and adapting your approach to serve their needs effectively.

Conclusion

> *"The best time to plant a tree was 20 years ago. The second best time is now. The same logic applies to turning your blog into a book, except trees don't generate royalties or speaking fees."* - Ancient proverb, updated for the digital age

You've been blogging for months or years, creating content that helps people solve problems, learn new skills, or see the world differently. That content represents thousands of hours of work and accumulated expertise that most people will never experience in organized, book-length form unless you make it happen.

The process isn't trivial. Converting blog content into a professional book requires strategic thinking, substantial new writing, careful editing, and attention to business details that most bloggers never consider. But it's also not as overwhelming as most people imagine. You already have the hardest part figured out: what to write about and how to communicate effectively with your audience.

Your blog has been your testing ground. You've learned which topics resonate, which explanations work, and which approaches your readers find most helpful. You've built credibility and demonstrated expertise in ways that would be impossible starting from scratch. Most importantly, you've proven that people value your perspective enough to return to your content repeatedly.

A book amplifies all these advantages while creating new opportunities that blogging alone can't provide. Books establish authority in ways that blog posts don't. They create revenue streams that can continue for years. They open doors to speaking, consulting, and media opportunities that might never have materialized otherwise.

But perhaps most importantly, a book gives you something tangible to point to when people ask what you do. Instead of explaining that you "write about marketing online," you can say you "wrote the book on email marketing for small businesses." That's a fundamentally different conversation starter.

The blog-to-book conversion process also makes you a better blogger. Organizing your scattered thoughts into coherent systems reveals gaps in your knowledge and inconsistencies in your thinking. The discipline required to create book-length content improves your ability to develop and express complex ideas. The research you do for your book generates material for months of future blog posts.

★ Pro Tip: Start thinking about your book project now, even if you're not ready to begin writing. The perspective shift from "blogger" to "author working on a book" changes how you approach your regular content creation.

Most bloggers who consider writing a book never start because they convince themselves they need more content, more credibility, or more time. The truth is that if you've been blogging consistently for six months or more, you probably have enough material to work with. If you've built an audience that engages with your content, you have validation that your expertise matters to other people.

The question isn't whether you have enough content or credentials to write a book. The question is whether you're willing to do the work required to organize that content into something valuable for readers who don't know you yet.

This book has given you the framework, but the execution is up to you. You can treat it as interesting information about a process you might try someday, or you can use it as a roadmap for a project you start this week. The difference between those two approaches is often the difference between bloggers who remain bloggers and bloggers who become authors.

Your content has value. Your expertise matters. Your perspective deserves a larger platform than your blog alone can provide. The only question remaining is what you're going to do about it.

The tools, platforms, and opportunities for independent publishing have never been better. The barriers that once prevented most people from becoming published authors have largely disappeared. What remains is the work itself: the strategic thinking, the writing, the editing, and the marketing that transforms good blog content into great books.

You already know how to create content that helps people. Now you know how to package that content in ways that can change your career, establish your authority, and create value that extends far beyond any individual blog post.

The rest is up to you.

About the Author

Richard Lowe brings authentic multi-domain expertise to the world of blog-to-book conversion, backed by 45 years of real-world experience spanning Fortune 500 technology leadership, professional ghostwriting, and creative excellence. As The Writing King, he has published 113+ books and helped clients secure millions in venture capital, land TEDx speaking opportunities, and transform careers from overlooked managers to recognized industry leaders.

Richard's unique background combines 20 years as Director of Computer Operations at Trader Joe's with expertise as a KnowBe4 Technical Editor, academic recognition through Purdue University textbook adoption, and a portfolio of 950,000+ professional photographs. This multi-domain authority allows him to serve clients that traditional specialists can't: biotech CEOs who need both technical knowledge and storytelling skills, tech executives requiring complex concept translation, and industry leaders who demand technical accuracy with compelling narrative.

His approach to content conversion draws from systems thinking developed through technology leadership, visual storytelling skills honed through professional photography, and the disciplined project management that comes from decades of enterprise operations. Richard has led digital transformations for billion-dollar companies, managed SCADA systems for major utilities, and pioneered fraud detection algorithms that became industry standards.

As a certified Community Emergency Response Team member who has survived three earthquakes over 7.1 magnitude, four hurricanes including a direct hit from Category 4 Hurricane Milton, and a forest fire that surrounded his vehicle with flames, Richard understands that real expertise comes from navigating challenges, not just theoretical knowledge.

His ghostwriting clients include Fortune 50 executives, platinum-selling rock stars, and tech entrepreneurs who have used their books into speaking fees ranging from $5,000 to $20,000 per keynote. Richard's book "Focus on LinkedIn" sold 15,000 copies in three days and has been professionally translated into seven languages. His work has been adopted as required reading at Purdue University's Krannert School of Management, where he regularly guest lectures.

Richard hosts the "Leaders and Their Stories" podcast and has appeared on 55+ shows including The Chris Voss Show, reaching over a million listeners. His comprehensive Code of Ethics and transparent business practices demonstrate the trustworthiness that separates genuine expertise from manufactured credentials.

When he's not helping clients transform their content into authority-building books, Richard develops his sixteen-book science fiction series "Peacekeeper," builds and paints miniature models, and explores caves and caverns across the American Southwest. He believes that every leader has a story worth telling and that the right book can change not just a career, but an entire industry.

Richard lives in Florida with his collection of unfinished creative projects and an unshakeable belief that the best time to turn your blog into a book was yesterday, but the second-best time is now.

Books by Richard Lowe

See books by Richard Lowe at

https://masterofworlds.com

Get free publishing insights and industry updates at

https://thewritingking.substack.com

For ghostwriting and book coaching services see

https://thewritingking.com

9 781946 458575